Cambridge English:
Business Vantage
5

WITH ANSWERS

Official examination papers from
University of Cambridge
ESOL Examinations

LEARNING CENTRE	
CLASS NO:	427 CAM ORANGE BOX
ACC NO:	106 833

CAMBRIDGE
UNIVERSITY PRESS

CAMBRIDGE UNIVERSITY PRESS
Cambridge, New York, Melbourne, Madrid, Cape Town,
Singapore, São Paulo, Delhi, Tokyo, Mexico City

Cambridge University Press
The Edinburgh Building, Cambridge CB2 8RU, UK

www.cambridge.org
Information on this title: www.cambridge.org/9781107664654

First published 2012

Printed in the United Kingdom at the University Press, Cambridge

A catalogue record for this book is available from the British Library

ISBN 978-1-107-66465-4 Student's Book with answers
ISBN 978-1-107-65472-3 Audio CD set
ISBN 978-1-107-60693-7 Self-study Pack

Cambridge University Press has no responsibility for the persistence or
accuracy of URLs for external or third-party internet websites referred to in
this publication, and does not guarantee that any content on such websites is,
or will remain, accurate or appropriate. Information regarding prices, travel
timetables and other factual information given in this work is correct at
the time of first printing but Cambridge University Press does not guarantee
the accuracy of such information thereafter.

Contents

Thanks and acknowledgements

Book design by Peter Ducker MSTD

Cover design by David Lawton

The CD which accompanies this book was recorded at dsound, London.

Introduction

TO THE STUDENT

This book is for candidates preparing for the Cambridge English: Business Vantage examination, also known as BEC Vantage. It contains four complete tests based on past papers.

Cambridge English: Business

Cambridge English: Business is a suite of certificated tests which can be taken on various dates throughout the year at approved Cambridge centres. They are aimed primarily at individual learners who wish to obtain a business-related English language qualification, and provide an ideal focus for courses in Business English. Set in a business context, Cambridge English: Business examinations test English language, not business knowledge.
The examinations are available at three levels – Preliminary, Vantage and Higher.

Cambridge English: Business is linked to the ALTE/Cambridge levels for language assessment, and to the Council of Europe's Framework of Reference for Languages. It is also aligned with the UK Qualifications and Curriculum Authority's National Standards for Literacy, within the National Qualifications Framework (NQF).

Business Exam	Equivalent Main Suite Exam	Council of Europe Framework Level	UK NQF Level
	Cambridge English: Proficiency *Certificate of Proficiency in English (CPE)*	C2 (ALTE Level 5)	
Business Higher	Cambridge English: Advanced *Certificate in Advanced English (CAE)*	C1 (ALTE Level 4)	Level 2*
Business Vantage	Cambridge English: First *First Certificate in English (FCE)*	B2 (ALTE Level 3)	Level 1
Business Preliminary	Cambridge English: Preliminary *Preliminary English Test (PET)*	B1 (ALTE Level 2)	Entry 3
	Cambridge English: Key *Key English Test (KET)*	A2 (ALTE Level 1)	

* This represents the level typically required for employment purposes to signify the successful completion of compulsory secondary education in the UK.

Business Vantage

The Business Vantage examination consists of four papers:

Reading	1 hour
Writing	45 minutes
Listening	40 minutes (approximately)
Speaking	14 minutes

Test of Reading (1 hour)

This paper consists of five parts with 45 questions, which take the form of two multiple-matching tasks, two multiple-choice tasks, and an error identification task. Part 1 contains four short texts or a longer text divided into four sections, and Parts 2, 3, 4 and 5 each contain one longer text. The texts are taken from newspapers, business magazines, business correspondence, books, leaflets, brochures, etc. They are all business-related, and are selected to test a wide range of reading skills and strategies.

Test of Writing (45 minutes)

For this paper, candidates are required to produce two pieces of writing. For Part 1, they write a note, message, memo or email to a colleague or colleagues within the company. For Part 2, they write a piece of business correspondence to somebody outside the company, a short report or a proposal. Candidates are asked to write 40 to 50 words for Part 1 and 120 to 140 words for Part 2.

Assessment is based on achievement of content, communication, organisation and language.

Test of Listening (approximately 40 minutes)

This paper consists of three parts with 30 questions, which take the form of a note-completion task, a multiple-matching task and a multiple-choice task. Part 1 contains three short conversations, Part 2 contains ten very short extracts, and Part 3 contains one longer text. The texts are audio recordings based on a variety of sources including interviews, telephone calls, face-to-face conversations and documentary features. They are all business-related, and are selected to test a wide range of listening skills and strategies.

Test of Speaking (14 minutes)

The Speaking test consists of three parts, which take the form of an interview section, a short presentation on a business topic, and a discussion. In the standard test format, candidates are examined in pairs by two examiners: an interlocutor and an assessor. The assessor awards a mark based on the following four criteria: Grammar and Vocabulary, Discourse Management, Pronunciation and Interactive Communication. The interlocutor provides a global mark for the whole test.

Marks and results

The four Vantage papers total 120 marks, after weighting. Each paper is weighted to 30 marks. A candidate's overall grade is based on the total score gained in all four papers. It is not necessary to achieve a satisfactory level in all four papers in order to pass the examination. Every candidate is provided with a Statement of Results, which includes a graphical display of their performance in each paper. These are shown against the scale Exceptional – Good – Borderline – Weak and indicate the candidate's relative performance in each paper.

TO THE TEACHER

Candidature

Each year Cambridge English: Business exams are taken by over 130,000 candidates throughout the world. Most candidates are either already in work or studying in preparation for the world of work.

Content, preparation and assessment

Material used throughout the Business exams is as far as possible authentic and free of bias, and reflects the international flavour of the examination. The subject matter should not advantage or disadvantage certain groups of candidates, nor should it offend in areas such as religion, politics or sex.

TEST OF READING

Part	Main Skill Focus	Input	Response	No. of Questions
1	Reading – scanning and gist	One longer or four shorter informational texts (approx. 250–350 words in total)	Matching	7
2	Reading – understanding text structure	Single text: article, report, etc. with sentence-length gaps (text plus seven option sentences approx. 450–550 words in total)	Matching	5
3	Reading for gist and specific information	Single text (approx. 450–550 words)	4-option multiple choice	6
4	Reading – vocabulary and structure information	Single informational text with lexical gaps (text including gapped words approx. 200–300 words)	4-option multiple-choice cloze	15
5	Reading – understanding sentence structure / error identification	Short text (150–200 words) Identification of additional unnecessary words in text	Proof-reading	12

Reading Part One

This is a matching task. There are four short texts on a related theme (for example, descriptions of a group of products, or advertisements for jobs) or a single text divided into four sections. Although the context of each text will be similar, there will also be information that is particular to each text. The texts are labelled A–D. Candidates are presented with a set of seven items which are statements related to the texts. They are expected to match each statement with the relevant text. Questions in this part tend to focus mostly on the identification of specific information and detail. However, an item could focus on gist by testing areas such as the target reader or the topic.

Preparation

In order to prepare for this part, it would be useful to familiarise students with sets of short texts that have a similar theme. Newspapers, magazines and catalogues are useful sources in which to find such texts. Students should be encouraged to look closely at all the information, particularly as short texts often include additional snippets of information on separate lines (such as prices, dates, titles, measurements, etc.) that can easily be overlooked.

Students could be set questions which test global reading skills prior to reading the texts, so that they are trained to think automatically for whom a text is written and why it has been written.

Reading Part Two

This is a matching task, comprising a text that has had six sentences removed from it and a set of seven sentences labelled A–G. Candidates are required to match each gap with the sentence which they think fits in terms of meaning and structure. The first gap is always given as an example so that candidates have five gaps left to complete. When they have finished this part, there will be one sentence left which they have not used.

The texts for this part will have been chosen because they have a clear line of thought or argument that can still be discerned by the reader even with the sentences removed. When doing the task, therefore, students should be trained to read through the gapped text and the list of sentences first, in order to get an idea of what it is about. Having done that, they should be reassured that there is only one sentence that fits each gap.

This part is a test of text structure as well as meaning, and the gaps will be reasonably far apart, so that candidates can successfully anticipate the appropriate lexical and grammatical features of the missing sentence. Candidates can be expected to be tested on a variety of cohesive features with both a backward and forward reference, sometimes going beyond the sentence level. Thus, while selecting the appropriate sentence for a gap, they should read before and after the text to ensure that it fits well. At the end of this part, they should read through the entire text, inserting the gapped sentences as they go along, to ensure that the information is coherent.

Preparation

This can be quite a difficult task, especially for candidates who are unfamiliar with such an exercise. In preparing them for this part, it would be a good idea to select a number of graded texts that have clear, familiar ideas and evident cohesive features. Texts can be cut up, as they are in the test, or simply discussed in their entirety. In this way, students can work up to dealing with more complex material and identifying the many different ways that ideas are connected. It would also be useful when doing gapped texts to look at sentences that do not fit the gaps and discuss the reasons for this. Sometimes it is possible to make a sentence fit a gap by simply changing a few words. Discussion on areas such as this would also be fruitful.

Reading Part Three

This task consists of a text accompanied by four-option multiple-choice items. The stem of a multiple-choice item may take the form of a question or an incomplete sentence. There are six items, which are placed after the text. The text is 450 to 550 words long. Sources of original texts may be the general and business press, company literature, and books on topics such as management. Texts may be edited, but the source is authentic.

Preparation

- Multiple-choice questions are a familiar and long-standing type of test; here, they are used to test opinion and inference rather than straightforward facts.
- Correct answers are not designed to depend on simple word-matching, and students' ability to interpret paraphrasing should be developed.
- Students should be encouraged to pursue their own interpretation of relevant parts of the text and then check their idea against the options offered, rather than reading all the options first.
- It could be useful for students to be given perhaps one of the wrong options only, and for them to try to write the correct answer and another wrong option.

Reading Part Four

This is a multiple-choice cloze test with 15 gaps, most of which test lexical items, and may focus on correct word choice, lexical collocations and fixed phrases. The texts chosen for this part will come from varied sources, but they will all have a straightforward message or meaning, so that candidates are being tested on vocabulary and not on their comprehension of the passage.

Preparation

Candidates are usually familiar with this type of task, and so it is most important to try and improve their range of vocabulary. The options provided in each item in the test will have similar meanings, but only one word will be correct within the context provided. Familiarity with typical collocations would be especially useful. The language of business is often very precise, and so it is worth spending time looking at the vocabulary used in different types of text, getting students to keep a vocabulary list and encouraging them to make active use of the lexical items that are new to them.

Reading Part Five

This is an error-correction or proof-reading task based on a text of 150 to 200 words, with 12 items. Candidates identify additional or unnecessary words in a text. This task can be related to the authentic task of checking a text for errors, and suitable text types are therefore letters, publicity materials, etc. The text is presented with 12 numbered lines, which are the lines containing the items. Further lines at the end may complete the text, but they are not numbered.

Preparation

- Students should be reminded that this task represents a kind of editing that is common practice, even in their first language.
- Any work on error analysis is likely to be helpful for this task.
- It may well be that photocopies of students' own writing could provide an authentic source for practice.
- A reverse of the exercise (giving students texts with missing words) might also prove beneficial.

Marks

One mark is given for each correct answer. The total score is then weighted to 30 marks for the whole Reading paper.

TEST OF WRITING

Part	Functions/Communicative Task	Input	Response	Register
1	e.g. giving instructions, explaining a development, asking for comments, requesting information, agreeing to requests	Rubric only (plus layout of output text type)	Internal communication (medium may be note, message, memo or email) (40–50 words)	Neutral/ informal
2	Report: describing, summarising Correspondence: e.g. explaining, apologising, reassuring, complaining Proposal: describing, summarising, recommending, persuading	One or more pieces of input from: business correspondence (medium may be letter, fax or email), internal communication (medium may be note, memo or email), notice, advert, graphs, charts, etc. (plus layout if output is fax or email)	Business correspondence (medium may be letter, fax or email) or short report or proposal (medium may be memo or email) (120–140 words)	Neutral/ formal

For Vantage, candidates are required to produce two pieces of writing:
- an internal company communication; this means a piece of communication with a colleague or colleagues within the company on a business-related matter, and the delivery medium may be a note, message, memo or email;
- one of the following:
  - a report; this means the presentation of information in relation to a specific issue or event. The report will contain an introduction, main body of findings and conclusion; it is possible that the delivery medium may be a memo or an email;
  - a piece of business correspondence; this means correspondence with somebody outside the company (e.g. a customer or supplier) on a business-related matter, and the delivery medium may be a letter, fax or email;
  - a proposal; this has a similar format to a report, but unlike the report, the focus of the proposal is on the future, with the main focus being on recommendations for discussion; it is possible that the delivery medium may be a memo or an email.

Writing Part One

In the first task, candidates are presented with the context in the task rubric. This explains the role the candidate must take in order to write a note, message, memo or email of around 40 to 50 words using a written prompt. It also identifies who the message is to be written to. The prompt will be included in the instructions in the rubric and will be in the form of bullet points clearly stating the pieces of information that must be incorporated into the answer.

Writing Part Two

In the second Writing task, candidates are required to write 120 to 140 words, which will be in the form of business correspondence, a short report or proposal. There will be an explanation of the task and one or more texts as input material. These texts may contain visual or graphic material, and have 'handwritten' notes on them.

Preparing for the Writing paper

Students should have practice in the clear and concise presentation of written information. Exposure to, and discussion of, as wide a range as possible of relevant texts would be beneficial. Students should be trained to consider:
- the target reader
- references to previous communication
- the purpose of writing
- the requirements of the format (e.g. letter, report)
- the main points to be addressed
- the approximate number of words to be written for each point
- suitable openings and closings
- the level of formality required.

It is important that students are aware of the need to reformulate the wording of the content points/handwritten notes given in the task, in order to include original vocabulary and structures, since evidence of a range of structures and vocabulary is one of the marking criteria.

Assessment

An impression mark is awarded to each piece of writing. Examiners look at four aspects of the candidate's writing: Content, Communicative Achievement, Organisation and Language.

Content focuses on how well the candidate has fulfilled the task, in other words if they have done what they were asked to do.
Communicative Achievement focuses on how appropriate the writing is and whether the appropriate register has been used.
Organisation focuses on the way the candidate put the piece of writing together, in other words if it is logical and ordered, and the punctuation is correct.
Language focuses on the use of vocabulary and grammar. This includes the range of language as well as how accurate it is.

For each of the criteria, the examiner gives a maximum of 5 marks. The band scores awarded are translated to a mark out of 10 for Part 1 and a mark out of 20 for Part 2. A total of 30 marks is available for Writing.

The general impression mark scheme is interpreted at Council of Europe Level B2.

Assessment Scale

B2	Content	Language	Organisation	Communicative Achievement
5	All content is relevant to the task. Target reader is fully informed.	Uses a range of everyday vocabulary appropriately, with occasional inappropriate use of less common lexis. Uses a range of simple and some complex grammatical forms with a good degree of control. Errors do not impede communication.	Text is generally well-organised and coherent, using a variety of linking words and cohesive devices.	Uses the conventions of the communicative task to hold the target reader's attention and communicate straightforward ideas.
4	*Performance shares features of Bands 3 and 5.*			
3	Minor irrelevances and/or omissions may be present. Target reader is on the whole informed.	Uses everyday vocabulary generally appropriately, while occasionally overusing certain lexis. Uses simple grammatical forms with a good degree of control. While errors are noticeable, meaning can still be determined.	Text is connected and coherent, using basic linking words and a limited number of cohesive devices.	Uses the conventions of the communicative task in generally appropriate ways to communicate straightforward ideas.
2	*Performance shares features of Bands 1 and 3.*			
1	Irrelevances and misinterpretation of task may be present. Target reader is minimally informed.	Uses basic vocabulary reasonably appropriately. Uses simple grammatical forms with some degree of control. Errors may impede meaning at times.	Text is connected using basic, high-frequency linking words.	Produces text that communicates simple ideas in simple ways.
0	Content is totally irrelevant. Target reader is not informed.	*Performance below Band 1.*		

Length of responses

Guidelines on length are provided for each task; responses which are too short may not have an adequate range of language and may not provide all the information that is required, while responses which are too long may contain irrelevant content and have a negative effect on the reader. These may affect candidates' marks on the relevant subscales.

Varieties of English

Candidates are expected to use a particular variety of English with some degree of consistency in areas such as spelling, and not for example switch from using a British spelling of a word to an American spelling of the same word.

TEST OF LISTENING

Part	Main Skill Focus	Input	Response	No. of Questions
1	Listening for writing short answers	Three telephone conversations or messages	Gap-filling	12
2	Listening; identifying topic, context, function, etc.	Short monologue; two sections of five 'snippets' each	Multiple matching	10
3	Listening	One extended conversation or monologue; interview, discussion, presentation, etc.	Multiple choice	8

Listening Part One

In this part, there are three conversations or answering-machine messages, with a gapped text to go with each. Each gapped text provides a very clear context and has four spaces which have to be filled with one or two words, or a number. The gapped texts may include forms, diary excerpts, invoices, message pads, etc. Candidates hear each conversation or message twice and as they listen they are required to complete the gapped text.

This part of the Listening test concentrates on the retrieval of factual information and it is important for candidates to listen carefully using the prompts on their question paper in order to identify the missing information. For example, they may have to note down a person's name, and if names on the recording are spelt out, those answers must be spelt correctly. Alternatively, they may have to listen for a room or telephone number, or an instruction or deadline. Answers to this part are rarely a simple matter of dictation and some reformulation of the prompt material will be required in order to locate the correct answer.

Listening Part Two

This part is divided into two sections. Each section has the same format: candidates hear five short monologues and have to match each monologue to a set of items, A–H. In each section, the eight options will form a coherent set and the overall theme or topic will be clearly stated in the task rubric. For example, candidates may hear five people talking and have to decide what sort of jobs the people do. Hence, the set of options A–H will contain a list of jobs. Alternatively, the set of options may consist of eight places/topics/addresses/purposes, etc. The two sections will always test different areas and so, if the first section focuses on, say, topics, the second section will focus on something else, such as functions.

In this part of the Listening test, candidates are being tested on their global listening skills and also on their ability to infer, extract gist and understand main ideas. In order to answer the questions successfully, they will need to work out the answer by developing ideas, and refining these as the text is heard. It will not be possible to 'word-match' and candidates should not expect to hear such overt cues. However, there will always be a 'right' answer and candidates are not expected to opt for the 'best' answer.

Listening Part Three

A longer text is heard in this part, usually lasting approximately four minutes. The text will typically be an interview, conversation or discussion with two or more speakers, or possibly a presentation or report with one speaker. There are eight, three-option multiple-choice questions that focus on details and main ideas in the text. There may be questions on opinions and feelings, but these will be relatively straightforward and will not require candidates to remember long or complex pieces of information.

Preparing for the Listening paper

All listening practice should be helpful for students, whether authentic or specially prepared. In particular, discussion should focus on:
- the purpose of speeches and conversations or discussions
- the speakers' roles
- the opinions expressed
- the language functions employed
- relevant aspects of phonology such as stress, linking and weak forms, etc.

In addition, students should be encouraged to appreciate the differing demands of each task type. It will be helpful not only to practise the task types in order to develop a sense of familiarity and confidence, but also to discuss how the three task types relate to real-life skills and situations:
- the first is note-taking (and therefore productive), and students should reflect on the various situations in which they take notes from a spoken input. They should also be encouraged to try to predict the kinds of words or numbers that might go in the gaps;
- the second is a matching (with discrimination) exercise, and reflects the ability to interrelate information between reading and listening and across differing styles and registers;
- the third involves the correct interpretation of spoken input, with correct answers often being delivered across different speakers.

In all three tasks, successful listening depends on correct reading, and students should be encouraged to make full use of the pauses during the test to check the written input.

Marks

One mark is given for each correct answer, giving a total score of 30 marks for the whole Listening paper.

TEST OF SPEAKING

Part	Format/Content	Time	Interaction Focus
1	Conversation between the interlocutor and each candidate Giving personal information; talking about present circumstances, past experiences and future plans, expressing opinions, speculating, etc.	About 3 minutes	The interlocutor encourages the candidates to give information about themselves and to express personal opinions.
2	A 'mini presentation' by each candidate on a business theme Organising a larger unit of discourse Giving information and expressing and justifying opinions	About 6 minutes	Each candidate is given prompts which they use to prepare and give a short talk on a business-related topic.
3	Two-way conversation between candidates followed by further prompting from the interlocutor Expressing and justifying opinions, speculating, comparing and contrasting, agreeing and disagreeing, etc.	About 5 minutes	The candidates are presented with a business-related situation to discuss. The interlocutor extends the discussion with prompts on related topics.

The test is conducted by two Speaking examiners (an interlocutor and an assessor), with pairs of candidates. The interlocutor is responsible for conducting the Speaking test and is also required to give a mark for each candidate's performance during the whole test. The assessor is responsible for providing an analytical assessment of each candidate's performance and, after being introduced by the interlocutor, takes no further part in the interaction.

The Speaking test is designed for pairs of candidates. However, where a centre has an uneven number of candidates, the last three candidates will be examined together.

Speaking Part One

In the first part of the test, the interlocutor addresses each candidate in turn and asks first general, then more business-related questions. Candidates will not be addressed in strict sequence. This part of the test takes about three minutes and during this time candidates are tested on their ability to talk briefly about themselves, and to perform functions such as agreeing and disagreeing, and expressing preferences.

Speaking Part Two

The second part of the test is a 'mini presentation'. In this part, the candidates are given a choice of topic and have a minute to prepare a presentation of approximately one minute. After each candidate has spoken, their partner is invited to ask a question about what has been said.

Speaking Part Three

The third part of the test is a discussion between candidates. The interlocutor gives candidates a business-related situation to discuss. The candidates are asked to speak for about three minutes. The interlocutor will support the conversation as appropriate and then ask further questions related to the main theme.

Preparing for the Speaking test

It is important to familiarise candidates with the format of the test before it takes place, by the use of paired and group activities in class. Teachers may need to explain the benefits of this type of assessment to candidates. The primary purpose of paired assessment is to sample a wider range of discourse than can be elicited from an individual interview.

In the first part of the test, candidates mainly respond to questions or comments from the interlocutor. Students need practice in exchanging personal and non-personal information; at Vantage level, it may be possible for students to practise talking about themselves in pairs or groups with or without prompts (such as written questions). However, prompt materials are necessary for Parts Two and Three, and students could be encouraged to design these themselves or may be provided with specially prepared sets. In small classes, students could discuss authentic materials as a group prior to engaging in pairwork or group activities. Such activities can familiarise students with the types of interactive skills involved in asking and providing factual information, such as: speaking clearly, formulating questions, listening carefully and giving precise answers.

In the 'mini presentation', candidates are asked to show an ability to talk for an extended period of time. Discussion activities, as well as giving short talks or presentations, can help to develop this skill.

In the final discussion in the Vantage Speaking test, candidates are also tested on their ability to express opinions, to compare and contrast, to concede points and possibly to reach a conclusion (although it is perfectly acceptable for candidates to agree to differ). Any discussion activities on a business theme that encourage students to employ these skills are likely to be beneficial. Group or class discussions can be valuable ways of developing these skills.

Assessment

Throughout the test candidates are assessed on their own individual performance and not in relation to the other candidate. They are assessed on their language skills, not on their personality, intelligence or knowledge of the world. Candidates must, however, be prepared to develop the conversation and respond to the tasks in an appropriate way.

Candidates are awarded marks by two examiners; the assessor and the interlocutor. The assessor awards marks by applying performance descriptors from the Analytical Assessment scales for the following criteria:

Grammar and Vocabulary

This refers to the accurate use of grammatical forms and appropriate use of vocabulary. It also includes the range of language.

Discourse Management

This refers to the extent, relevance and coherence of each candidate's contributions. Candidates should be able to construct clear stretches of speech which are easy to follow. The length of their contributions should be appropriate to the task, and what they say should be related to the topic and the conversation in general.

Pronunciation

This refers to the intelligibility of contributions at word and sentence levels. Candidates should be able to produce utterances that can easily be understood, and which show control of intonation, stress and individual sounds.

Interactive Communication

This refers to the ability to use language to achieve meaningful communication. Candidates should be able to initiate and respond appropriately according to the task and conversation, and also to use interactive strategies to maintain and develop the communication whilst negotiating towards an outcome.

B2	Grammar and Vocabulary	Discourse Management	Pronunciation	Interactive Communication
5	• Shows a good degree of control of a range of simple and some complex grammatical forms. • Uses a range of appropriate vocabulary to give and exchange views on a wide range of familiar topics.	• Produces extended stretches of language with very little hesitation. • Contributions are relevant and there is a clear organisation of ideas. • Uses a range of cohesive devices and discourse markers.	• Is intelligible. • Intonation is appropriate. • Sentence and word stress is accurately placed. • Individual sounds are articulated clearly.	• Initiates and responds appropriately, linking contributions to those of other speakers. • Maintains and develops the interaction and negotiates towards an outcome.
4	*Performance shares features of Bands 3 and 5.*			
3	• Shows a good degree of control of simple grammatical forms, and attempts some complex grammatical forms. • Uses a range of appropriate vocabulary to give and exchange views on a range of familiar topics.	• Produces extended stretches of language despite some hesitation. • Contributions are relevant and there is very little repetition. • Uses a range of cohesive devices.	• Is intelligible. • Intonation is generally appropriate. • Sentence and word stress is generally accurately placed. • Individual sounds are generally articulated clearly.	• Initiates and responds appropriately. • Maintains and develops the interaction and negotiates towards an outcome with very little support.
2	*Performance shares features of Bands 1 and 3.*			
1	• Shows a good degree of control of simple grammatical forms. • Uses a range of appropriate vocabulary when talking about everyday situations.	• Produces responses which are extended beyond short phrases, despite hesitation. • Contributions are mostly relevant, despite some repetition. • Uses basic cohesive devices.	• Is mostly intelligible, and has some control of phonological features at both utterance and word levels.	• Initiates and responds appropriately. • Keeps the interaction going with very little prompting and support.
0	*Performance below Band 1.*			

The interlocutor awards a mark for overall performance using a Global Achievement scale.

B2	Global Achievement
5	• Handles communication on a range of familiar topics, with very little hesitation. • Uses accurate and appropriate linguistic resources to express ideas and produce extended discourse that is generally coherent.
4	*Performance shares features of Bands 3 and 5.*
3	• Handles communication on familiar topics, despite some hesitation. • Organises extended discourse but occasionally produces utterances that lack coherence, and some inaccuracies and inappropriate usage occur.
2	*Performance shares features of Bands 1 and 3.*
1	• Handles communication in everyday situations, despite hesitation. • Constructs longer utterances but is not able to use complex language except in well-rehearsed utterances.
0	*Performance below Band 1.*

Assessment for Vantage is based on performance across all parts of the test, and is achieved by applying the relevant descriptors in the assessment scales.

Grading and results

Grading takes place once all scripts have been returned to Cambridge ESOL and marking is complete. This is approximately five weeks after the examination. There are two main stages: grading and awards.

Grading

The four papers total 120 marks, after weighting. Each skill represents 25% of the total marks available. The grade boundaries (A, B, C, B1) are set using the following information:
● statistics on the candidature
● statistics on the overall candidate performance
● statistics on individual items, for those parts of the examination for which this is appropriate (Reading and Listening)
● the advice of the Principal Examiners, based on the performance of candidates, and on the recommendation of examiners where this is relevant (Writing)
● comparison with statistics from previous years' examination performance and candidature.
A candidate's overall grade is based on the total score gained in all four papers. It is not necessary to achieve a satisfactory level in all four papers in order to pass the examination.

Awards

The Awarding Committee deals with all cases presented for special consideration, e.g. temporary disability, unsatisfactory examination conditions, suspected collusion, etc. The Committee can decide to ask for scripts to be re-marked, to check results, to change grades, to withhold results, etc. Results may be withheld because of infringement of regulations or because further investigation is needed. Centres are notified if a candidate's results have been scrutinised by the Awarding Committee.

Results

Exceptional candidates sometimes show ability beyond B2 level. Candidates who achieve grade A receive the Business English Certificate Vantage stating that they demonstrated ability at Level C1. Candidates who achieve grade B or C receive the Business English Certificate Vantage at Level B2. Candidates whose performance is below B2 level, but falls within Level B1, receive a Cambridge English certificate stating that they have demonstrated ability at B1 level. Candidates whose performance falls below Level B1 do not receive a certificate.

Further information

For more information about Cambridge English: Business tests or any other Cambridge ESOL examination, write to:

University of Cambridge ESOL Examinations
1 Hills Road
Cambridge
CB1 2EU
United Kingdom

Tel: +44 1223 553997
Fax: +44 1223 553621
email: ESOLHelpdesk@ucles.org.uk
website: www.CambridgeESOL.org

In some areas, this information can also be obtained from the British Council.

Test 1

READING   1 hour

PART ONE

Questions 1–7

- Look at the statements below and the information on the opposite page about feedback on staff performance.
- Which section (**A**, **B**, **C** or **D**) does each statement **1–7** refer to?
- For each statement (**1–7**), mark one letter (**A**, **B**, **C** or **D**) on your Answer Sheet.
- You will need to use some of these letters more than once.

Example:

0   the reluctance of companies to base pay on staff feedback

0	A	B	C	D
	▭	▭	▭	▬

---

1   staff being reminded that it is not essential to restrict feedback to once a year

2   the way in which feedback could identify people suitable for promotion

3   the aim of improving staff communication throughout an organisation

4   the feedback obtained on an employee being linked to requirements for a particular job

5   aspects of a group of employees' work that were identified as requiring improvement

6   feedback indicating both positive and negative aspects of an individual's work

7   the participation of less senior personnel in a member of staff's feedback

Changes in Performance Feedback

A   In the past, feedback about your performance used to mean a quiet chat with the boss. But now 360-degree feedback – the system where employees are also given feedback from peers and from the people they manage – is taking root in corporate culture. The system is characterised by greater participation and has grown out of the desire of companies to create more open working environments where people work better together and ideas and opinions are exchanged between teams and across levels of seniority.

B   PCs linked to the company IT network are set to become the feedback machines. Many firms introducing 360-degree feedback are using Personal Development Planner software. Feedback on an individual, which is based on a questionnaire relating to attributes needed for that person's role in the company, is collected using this electronic system. All the information gathered is analysed and the end result is a suggested development plan. The advantage is that individuals make requests for the feedback themselves and receive the results directly.

C   Sarah Rains, from the pharmaceutical company Optec, said, 'Now feedback is available on our network, we encourage managers to choose how they use it. It is a flexible tool and we tell them that waiting for the annual event of a formal appraisal needn't apply.' At the engineering company NT, 250 technical managers have been through the feedback process. Jack Palmer, a senior manager there said, 'We needed to develop the interpersonal skills of these technically-minded people. In particular, we wanted to build on their team-working and coaching skills.'

D   So, how is the new feedback culture likely to affect you? It could form the basis of your personal development programme, providing pointers to your strengths and also to those areas you need to develop more. Or feedback could be used for 'succession planning', where companies use the information to speculate on who has the right skills to move into more senior positions. As yet, few organisations have stretched the role of feedback so far as to link it to salaries. But one thing is clear: the future will bring even wider participation by all members of staff.

HARROW COLLEGE
Learning Centre

PART TWO

Questions 8–12

- Read the article below about working in international teams.
- Choose the best sentence from the opposite page to fill each of the gaps.
- For each gap (**8–12**), mark one letter (**A–G**) on your Answer Sheet.
- Do not use any letter more than once.
- There is an example at the beginning (**0**).

INTERNATIONAL TEAMS

An international team can be defined as a group of people who come from different nationalities and work together towards a common goal. (**0**) .....G..... The fact that they are spread out presents a range of opportunities and challenges that teams working in the same place do not experience.

One trend, in particular, which is creating the need for more international teams, is that we are in the middle of a dramatic information revolution. (**8**) .... Thus, these teams can now spend as much time working apart as together. They can access and share information as never before. Business will increasingly be done in an 'information space', with information becoming a product in its own right. (**9**) .... Doing this through the internet and e-mail is inexpensive and relatively easy, in both technologically developed and developing countries.

A question commonly asked by managers is whether these teams actually work. Can they deliver improved performance? After a decade of work experience and research with international teams, I believe the answer is positive. (**10**) .... What's more, many of those companies which have actually introduced international teams have focused only on the performance of the teams, without taking into account the context in which they are introduced. Context plays a key role in the likelihood of their success.

Creating the right context for international teams needs more than a quick fix, though. It requires a long-term commitment. (**11**) .... On the contrary, companies need to focus on the way they operate, and possibly initiate a complete review of their practices, before introducing an international team.

Given these challenges, what should organisations do to make sure that their international teams are successful? Much has been written about effective team processes in general, and the first thing to say is that most of these guidelines apply equally to international teams. Experience has shown that international teams are simply more complex versions of national teams. (**12**) .... While these elements may have a variety of interpretations in different cultures, they are as important to international teams as they are to national teams.

A   If an organisation is just beginning to work globally and has only recently created international teams, it often underestimates the level of support needed by teams.

B   It is now well established that any team will have a greater chance of success if it has clear goals, a strong sense of commitment, appropriate leadership and good interpersonal relationships.

C   The recognition of this has created many more knowledge workers, that is, people who create, exchange and broadcast information as knowledge.

D   Organisations must understand that operating globally affects every aspect of business and they cannot simply set up international teams and assume that everything else can remain unchanged.

E   The first major impact of this is that satellite technology is increasingly allowing team members to participate in discussions wherever they are, at any time they choose.

F   Unfortunately, however, few organisations until now have been prepared to make the necessary investment to gain the potential benefits that international teams offer.

G   Unlike most national teams, international teams often work apart and across cultures and time zones, for extended periods of time.

PART THREE

Questions 13–18

- Read the article below about leadership in business and the questions on the opposite page.
- For each question (**13–18**), mark one letter (**A, B, C** or **D**) on your Answer Sheet.

═══ THE EFFECTIVE LEADER ═══

From workplace surveys, I have found that most people want to be – and feel they could be – more effective leaders. Certainly they want their leaders to be more effective. But what do we mean by effective leadership in business? It would appear a simple question. Unfortunately, effectiveness is more easily recognisable when it is absent. Leaders who attempt to use business jargon and try out the latest ideas are too often perceived as figures of fun. Whilst people frequently agree on what ineffective leadership is, clearly knowing what not to do is hardly helpful in practice.

Huge amounts of research have been done on this very wide subject. When you look at leadership in different ways, you see different things. While descriptions of leadership are all different, they are all true – and this is where disagreement arises. However, leadership is specific to a given context. The effectiveness of your actions is assessed in relation to the context and to the conditions under which you took them.

For a magazine article I wrote recently, I interviewed one publishing executive, author of several well-known publications, about what effective leadership is. It was significant that, at first, he did not mention his own company. He talked at length about what was happening in the industry – the mergers, take-overs and global nature of the business. Before he was able to describe his own objectives for the new publishing organisation he was setting up, he had to see a clear fit between these proposals and the larger situation outside. Obvious? Of course. But I have lost count of the number of leaders I have coached who believed that their ideas were valid, whatever the situation.

At this point, I should also mention another example, that of a finance director whose plan of action was not well received. The company he had joined had grown steadily for twenty years, serving clients who were in the main distrustful of any product that was too revolutionary. The finance director saw potential challenges from competitors and wanted his organisation to move with the times. Unfortunately, most staff below him were unwilling to change. I concluded that although there were certainly some personal skills he could improve upon, what he most needed to do was to communicate effectively with his subordinates, so that they all felt at ease with his different approach.

Some effective leaders believe they can control uncertainty because they know what the organisation should be doing and how to do it. Within the organisation itself, expertise is usually greatly valued, and executives are expected, as they rise within the system, to know more than those beneath them and, therefore, to manage the operation. A good example of this would be a firm of accountants I visited. Their business was built on selling reliable expertise to the client, who naturally wants uncertainty to be something only other companies have to face. Within this firm, giving the right answer was greatly valued, and mistakes were clearly to be avoided.

I am particularly interested in what aims leaders have and what their role should be in helping the organisation achieve its strategic aims. Some leaders are highly ineffective when the aim doesn't fit with the need, such as the manufacturing manager who was encouraged by her bosses to make revolutionary changes. She did, and was very successful. However, when she moved to a different part of the business, she carried on her programme of change. Unfortunately, this part of the business had already suffered badly from two mismanaged attempts at change. My point is that what her people needed at that moment was a steady hand, not further changes – she should have recognised that. The outcome was that within six months staff were calling for her resignation.

13 In the first paragraph, the writer says that poor leaders

    A do not want to listen to criticism.
    B do not deserve to be taken seriously.
    C are easier to identify than good ones.
    D are more widespread than people think.

14 Why does the writer believe there is disagreement about what effective leadership is?

    A Definitions of successful leadership vary according to the situation.
    B There are few examples of outstanding leaders available to study.
    C Leaders are unable to give clear descriptions of their qualities.
    D The results of research on the subject have concluded little.

15 The publishing executive's priorities for leadership focused on

    A significant and long-term aims.
    B internal organisational aspects.
    C professional skills and abilities.
    D overall business contexts.

16 According to the writer, the finance director was unsuccessful because

    A staff were uncomfortable with his style.
    B existing clients were suspicious of change.
    C competitors had a more dynamic approach.
    D colleagues gave little support to his ideas.

17 Staff at the accountancy firm who were promoted were required to

    A correct mistakes.
    B have a high level of knowledge.
    C maintain discipline within the organisation.
    D advise clients on responding to uncertainty.

18 The example of the manager at the manufacturing company is given to emphasise that

    A managers need support from their employers.
    B leaders should not be afraid of being unpopular.
    C effective leaders must be sensitive to staff needs.
    D managers do not always understand the attitudes of staff.

PART FOUR

Questions 19–33

- Read the extract below from the annual report of a company with manufacturing interests around the world.
- Choose the best word to fill each gap from **A**, **B**, **C** or **D** on the opposite page.
- For each question (**19–33**), mark one letter (**A**, **B**, **C** or **D**) on your Answer Sheet.
- There is an example at the beginning (**0**).

Manufacturing Strategy

During the last year, we announced the significant (**0**) .....B..... of our plastic sheeting plant in Malaysia, which, together with the acquisition of the Javanese factory, will approximately double the Group's manufacturing (**19**) .... The cost of this development is within (**20**) .... and will be approximately $5.6m, of which $2.7m was incurred during the previous year. It is on schedule to (**21**) .... increasing volumes from October 2009.

Following the (**22**) .... of plastic tubing manufacture from Germany to Thailand, we have effectively doubled the capacity of this facility at an (**23**) .... cost of $12m. The project is set to cost less than the original (**24**) .... and is on target for increased production by June 2010.

In February, we announced our (**25**) .... to sell our factory in Ireland. This decision is in line with the Group's strategy of (**26**) .... on our core categories of branded products.

In June, we announced investment in a new state-of-the-art UK manufacturing facility for specialist plastic components. This facility will be (**27**) .... by mid 2009 and will increase the Group's capacity to manufacture products efficiently in-house. At the same time it will (**28**) .... about 200 new jobs in an area of high unemployment. The factory is to cost approximately $24m, towards which government (**29**) .... of up to $4m are already available. Sadly, as part of this move, we announced the (**30**) .... of our Blackburn facility, which is due to take place in the early part of 2010.

As part of our commitment to effective external communications with all our stakeholders, in October we (**31**) .... the corporate website, which is now providing up-to-date information on the Group and we look forward to receiving (**32**) .... from users of the site. Existing product websites are now in the (**33**) .... of being redesigned as part of the global rebranding strategy.

Example:

| | A | extension | B | expansion | C | accumulation | D | inflation |

	A B C D
0	☐ ■ ☐ ☐

19	**A** output	**B** yield	**C** total	**D** mass
20	**A** budget	**B** income	**C** account	**D** fund
21	**A** forward	**B** transfer	**C** advance	**D** deliver
22	**A** replacement	**B** rearranging	**C** relocation	**D** redistribution
23	**A** aimed	**B** imagined	**C** accepted	**D** expected
24	**A** guess	**B** judgement	**C** estimate	**D** conviction
25	**A** focus	**B** object	**C** intention	**D** purpose
26	**A** concentrating	**B** planning	**C** attending	**D** directing
27	**A** running	**B** implementing	**C** executing	**D** organizing
28	**A** appoint	**B** result	**C** employ	**D** create
29	**A** scholarships	**B** grants	**C** allocations	**D** gifts
30	**A** finish	**B** closure	**C** ending	**D** conclusion
31	**A** dispatched	**B** prompted	**C** launched	**D** effected
32	**A** attitude	**B** approach	**C** outlook	**D** feedback
33	**A** practice	**B** progress	**C** process	**D** procedure

PART FIVE

Questions 34–45

- Read the article below about market research.
- In most of the lines (**34–45**), there is one extra word. It is either grammatically incorrect or does not fit in with the meaning of the text. Some lines, however, are correct.
- If a line is correct, write **CORRECT** on your Answer Sheet.
- If there is an extra word in the line, write **the extra word** in CAPITAL LETTERS on your Answer Sheet.
- The exercise begins with two examples (**0** and **00**).

Examples:

| 0 | I | N | | | | | | | |

| 00 | C | O | R | R | E | C | T | | |

Market Research

0 Market research involves in collecting and sorting facts and opinions from specific groups

00 of people. The purpose of research can vary from discovering the popularity of a political

34 party to assessing whether is a product needs changing or replacing. Most work in

35 consumer research involves interviewers employed by market research agencies, but

36 certain industrial and social research is carried out by any specialist agencies. Interviews

37 may be with individuals or groups and can last anything as from minutes to an hour or

38 more. In some interviews, people may be asked to examine or try out products before

39 giving up their opinion. Successful interviewers tend to like meeting people and should not

40 only be shy of addressing strangers. Interviewers are usually expected to work

41 unsupervised, organising their own workload. Self-discipline is absolutely essential – and

42 as are good health and energy. There are no specific age limits for such a work though

43 many agencies prefer to employ older applicants with experience of meeting people.

44 Market research agencies which frequently organise training, where trainees learn how to

45 recognise socio-economic groups and practise approaching to the public. For information

on market research training and qualifications, contact the Market Research Association.

WRITING   45 minutes

PART ONE

- You are a manager in an international company. You want to reduce the company's spending on courier services.
- Write an **email** to the staff in your department:
  - explaining that spending on courier services has risen
  - suggesting how savings could be made
  - saying how the money saved will be used.
- Write **40–50** words.

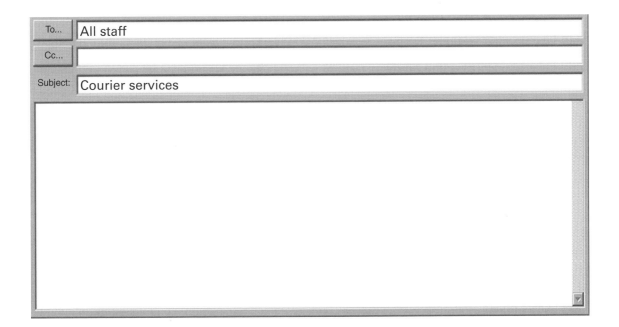

To...	All staff
Cc...	
Subject:	Courier services

PART TWO

- You are a manager in the customer services department of a large store. Your line manager has asked you to write a report on the results of a recent customer survey.
- Look at the information below, on which you have already made some handwritten notes.
- Then, using **all** your handwritten notes, write your **report**.
- Write **120–140** words.

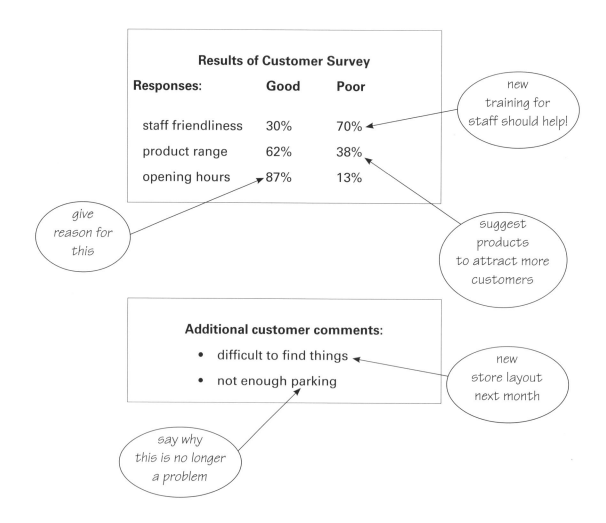

LISTENING   40 minutes (including 10 minutes' transfer time)

PART ONE

Questions 1–12

- You will hear three telephone conversations or messages.
- Write **one or two words or a number** in the numbered spaces on the notes or forms below.
- After you have listened once, replay each recording.

Conversation One

(Questions 1–4)

- Look at the note below.
- You will hear a man calling his office.

Telephone message

Martin Hayes phoned from the **(1)** ....

There's a problem: the **(2)** .... haven't

arrived! (They were sent by air last week.)

Another thing: he needs more **(3)** ....

He's attending a **(4)** .... this morning,

so call him back around lunchtime.

Conversation Two

(Questions 5–8)

- Look at the note below.
- You will hear a woman calling about a job application.

MESSAGE FOR JILL

Sara (5) .... called this morning

about the post of (6) ....

They'd like you to attend a (7) ....

on the 28th; they'll confirm this by letter.

In the meantime, can you send her details of your

(8) ....

Conversation Three

(Questions 9–12)

- Look at the note below.
- You will hear a man phoning about some arrangements for a meeting.

While you were out

Message for: *Lauren O'Neil* **From:** *Chris Darcy*

Message

Chris (HR) phoned about meeting of

(9) .... *next week.*

There's going to be an announcement about

(10) ....

MD wants you to make presentation on

(11) .... *of the new company.*

Could you also cover **(12)** .... *in your presentation? If any questions, call Chris directly.*

PART TWO

Questions 13–22

Section One

(Questions 13–17)

- You will hear five short recordings.
- For each recording, decide which aspect of working conditions the speaker is talking about.
- Write **one** letter (**A–H**) next to the number of the recording.
- Do not use any letter more than once.
- After you have listened once, replay the recordings.

13	....	**A**	career prospects
		B	health and safety
14	....	**C**	working hours
15	....	**D**	holiday allowance
		E	training courses
16	....	**F**	disciplinary procedures
		G	job security
17	....	**H**	pay increases

Section Two

(Questions 18–22)

- You will hear another five recordings.
- For each recording, decide what each speaker is trying to do.
- Write **one** letter (**A–H**) next to the number of the recording.
- Do not use any letter more than once.
- After you have listened once, replay the recordings.

18	....	**A**	nominate a supplier
		B	present sales figures
19	....	**C**	support a proposal
20	....	**D**	refuse an increment
		E	agree to expenditure
21	....	**F**	claim damages
		G	negotiate a contract
22	....	**H**	request a postponement

PART THREE

Questions 23–30

- You will hear a radio interview with a leading industrialist and business consultant, Philip Spencer.
- For each question (**23–30**), mark one letter (**A**, **B** or **C**) for the correct answer.
- After you have listened once, replay the recording.

23 When visiting companies Philip Spencer's objective is to

  A improve staff productivity.
  B identify problem areas.
  C re-train weak management.

24 Problems at Manson's had continued after Spencer's first visit because of

  A poor distribution systems.
  B inadequate market research.
  C out-dated production methods.

25 Difficulties at Criterion Glass stemmed from lack of attention to

  A competitors' designs.
  B quality of merchandise.
  C consumer demand.

26 Philip Spencer blames his early business difficulties on

  A inexperience with new companies.
  B lack of knowledge of the financial sector.
  C bad advice from established organisations.

27 He defends his unusual personal style by saying that

  A it is important in business to make a strong impression.
  B his business ideas are more important than his appearance.
  C most business people are too serious and traditional.

28 He thinks he was appointed chairman of LBI because the company

  A knew of his successes with failing companies.
  B felt he had a positive image with the public.
  C liked his fearless approach to problem-solving.

29 According to Philip Spencer, successful managers are distinguished by their

    A concern for detail.
    B desire to make money.
    C strong leadership.

30 His final advice to people starting in business is to

    A make every effort to prevent mistakes.
    B find the best sources of information.
    C maintain a positive attitude at all times.

You now have 10 minutes to transfer your answers to your Answer Sheet.

SPEAKING   14 minutes

SAMPLE SPEAKING TASKS

PART ONE

In this part, the interlocutor asks questions to each of the candidates in turn. You have to give information about yourself and express personal opinions.

PART TWO

In this part of the test, you are asked to give a short talk on a business topic. You have to choose one of the topics from the three below and then talk for about one minute. You have one minute to prepare your ideas.

A: What is important when . . . ?

Writing a newspaper advertisement for a job vacancy
- Description of the work
- Experience needed by applicants
-
-

B: What is important when . . . ?

Selecting employees for further training
- Commitment to company
- Previous training
-
-

C: What is important when . . . ?

Planning corporate hospitality
- Guest list
- Type of event
-
-

PART THREE

In this part of the test, you are given a discussion topic. You have 30 seconds to look at the task prompt, an example of which is below, and then about three minutes to discuss the topic with your partner. After that, the examiner will ask you more questions related to the topic.

For **two** candidates

Video Conferencing

The company you work for is concerned about the amount of time staff spend travelling to meetings in other branches of the company, and is looking at alternatives.

You have been asked to make recommendations about introducing video conferencing.

Discuss the situation together and decide:

- what the company needs to know about the meetings that take place at present

- what the advantages and disadvantages of video conferencing might be.

For **three** candidates

Video Conferencing

The company you work for is concerned about the amount of time staff spend travelling to meetings in other branches of the company, and is looking at alternatives.

You have been asked to make recommendations about introducing video conferencing.

Discuss the situation together and decide:

- what the company needs to know about the meetings that take place at present

- what the advantages and disadvantages of video conferencing might be

- what kinds of practical preparations would be needed before introducing the system.

Follow-on questions

- Would you prefer to have meetings face-to-face or through video conferencing? (Why?)

- In what other ways do you think a company could reduce the need for travelling to meetings? (Why?)

- What do you think are the benefits to staff of business travel? (Why?)

- Do you think modern technology has affected the amount of business travel in recent years? (Why?/Why not?)

- Do you think video conferencing will become more important for meetings in the future? (Why?/Why not?)

Test 2

READING   1 hour

PART ONE

Questions 1–7

- Look at the statements below and the advice of four market analysts about a company's future strategy on the opposite page.
- Which analyst's advice (**A, B, C** or **D**) does each statement (**1–7**) refer to?
- For each statement (**1–7**), mark one letter (**A, B, C** or **D**) on your Answer Sheet.
- You will need to use some of these letters more than once.

Example:

0   It would be inadvisable for Dexter to extend its range of products at this time.

---

1   The kind of promotion Dexter has relied on so far is unlikely to influence its target customers.

2   Although Dexter can probably extend its range, finding enough capital will be difficult.

3   Dexter needs to think carefully about the brand image of its products.

4   Supplying niche retailers could give Dexter access to a new group of customers.

5   Dexter should consider working with a company experienced in advertising on a large scale.

6   Increasing the margin on the current range is an area Dexter should concentrate on.

7   Dexter's approach to doing business has enabled it to compete with larger companies.

What next for Dexter?

Dexter's new shaving cream is a hit in the UK. The company's next challenges are to branch out into new products and to succeed in America. Four top analysts give their advice.

A

Joe Hutchinson

For Dexter, the hardest part is yet to come. Many British companies fail in the U.S. and Dexter is, unsurprisingly, finding it tough. And what's the sense in seeking cash for expansion into new product areas while having to support a loss-making American operation? There are more important things to do with the money, for example dealing with the company's low profitability – a 2% return on sales. It might well be time to look at a few cost headings.

B

Dan Valero

Breaking out of the shaving cream market should not be impossible for Dexter, but raising the money to launch the products is the real challenge. Dexter might seek a partner with the promotional skills needed for mass marketing, or focus on product development and franchising. They ought to consider whether they should continue to attack the American market, and, if so, they should seek a local partner. If control is a priority, the European market may be worth a look instead.

C

James Sunderland

Dexter's entrepreneurship, which has helped it get a share of a market previously dominated by two players, will be the key to further growth. The American market is particularly challenging, but a possible strategy is to target distributors to American retailers or a British-based subsidiary of an American parent. Another approach may be to form alliances with like-minded cult fashion or sports outlets and attract a slice of the US market open to trying new products.

D

Melanie Laconte

Dexter intends to increase its market share, and one way of doing this is to introduce new products, perhaps aimed at women, into its existing range. However, its managers must be aware that the women's grooming market is crowded, and that to extend here they must remain loyal to the values of their existing range while still proving attractive to the new sector. They need to take a hard look at how to generate demand; so far it's worked well through word of mouth but the average American buyer expects a huge advertising campaign.

PART TWO

Questions 8–12

- Read the article below about developments at a bank.
- Choose the best sentence from the opposite page to fill each of the gaps.
- For each gap (**8–12**), mark one letter (**A–G**) on your Answer Sheet.
- Do not mark any letter more than once.
- There is an example at the beginning (**0**).

The Pan-Slavic Trading Bank

When Miroslav Novak started work as a graduate trainee, his employer, the Pan-Slavic Trading Bank (P-STB), was a state-owned bank specialising in export trade. Though only the country's fourth bank in size and turnover, it was well run and had a proven track record. (**0**) .....G..... Despite its inclusion in the government's programme of privatisation, expansion or major change were not on the agenda.

Today, ten years on, Miroslav has come a long way from his modest beginnings. Recently appointed director of the branch network, he now sits on the executive board. (**8**) .... Of particular concern is the fact that the P-STB has become a retail bank, no longer dealing exclusively with large companies. This sector has, in fact, been downgraded to secondary status, since the most important market is seen to be elsewhere.

The new emphasis is on offering a wide range of products to the general public. (**9**) .... When this policy was first put forward, Miroslav and his colleagues doubted its feasibility, since it was not part of their financial culture. The directors went ahead with their plans, however, and, as success followed success, their doubting employees were forced to admit to having been mistaken.

The source of the P-STB's change of direction was to be found abroad; the direc-

tors of a bank from Luxembourg had been monitoring the progress of the P-STB as it moved towards privatisation. (**10**) .... After lengthy negotiations, including with government departments, the Luxembourg bank was successful and became the majority shareholder. The P-STB now found itself the subsidiary of a foreign bank.

No time was wasted in flying in a team of managers from the parent company. No sooner had they arrived than major changes began to be implemented. (**11**) .... This was exciting and challenging, but there was a high price to pay. The average working day increased from eight to twelve hours almost immediately, and several of the longer-serving staff were given early retirement. Those who remained felt extremely uncomfortable about the contrast in their fortunes.

The next few months under new ownership were extremely demanding and Miroslav found little to be optimistic about. (**12**) .... Miroslav grew to enjoy the demands made on him, and before long was promoted to his present position, with responsibility for converting all the branches in the network to retail banking. He spends less time than he would like with his family, and still misses former colleagues, but the work itself is more satisfying than he could ever have imagined.

Example:

A   Liking what they saw, they put in a bid, in fierce competition with at least five other financial institutions.

B   Despite this, and although he is one of the relatively few to have prospered, he feels that his position is far from secure.

C   Gradually, though, as the new structure took shape, the bank began to feel like a modern company with an exciting future.

D   Young employees were given responsible positions, including Miroslav, who was put in charge of a department.

E   The bank has, in effect, become a financial supermarket, where customers can purchase the services they need 'off the shelf'.

F   They decided that it was the right moment to exploit this area of weakness.

G   With a client base restricted to national corporations, for whom it financed overseas trade, the P-STB put its success down to reliability and conservatism.

PART THREE

Questions 13–18

- Read the article below about careers in children's book publishing and the questions on the opposite page.
- For each question (**13–18**), mark one letter (**A**, **B**, **C** or **D**) on your Answer Sheet.

Leading from the top

Catherine Bauer looks at career development in children's book publishing

To get on in the world of children's book publishing one needs to be 'bright, nice and not ambitious'. Those are the words of a 37-year-old manager thinking about leaving the industry. Managers in other industries would, by that age, be striving towards greater leadership challenges and rewards, while Human Resources departments would be doing all they could to prevent hungry competitors from getting hold of experienced and talented employees. Maintaining successful corporations and happy shareholders is, after all, dependent on using the talents and experience of one's staff, not on being nice.

Career progression in the children's sector of publishing seems to be determined almost by luck rather than a proper career structure or assessment of employees' competencies. Sarah Carter, for example, started her career as an assistant in the customer service department at William Davis Publishing. She only became aware of a vacancy in public relations because her department was on the same floor as the publicity office. 'I had already been promoted to manager in my department, but realised that any career development there would be limited. I decided to move sideways into PR, which was also where I felt my skills were more suited. I was lucky a position came up within the company.'

Across the publishing houses, staff training or development is generally dependent on the approach taken by your immediate boss. Virginia Coutts, editorial director at Prodigy Publications, says, 'This is fine, if you happen to have one who is effective. When I started at Prodigy I worked for Roger Gibbons. I was in children's fiction, but he also gave me some work on picture books and non-fiction, and that meant I gained experience in a range of areas. He also made sure that new people didn't come in, train and then move on. And it wasn't a question of being here for three years or so before you got promoted.'

Not everyone has a similar experience with their manager, but this is not surprising when one considers that few managers have themselves had any structured training. Mark Harlock, marketing manager at T R Publishers, says, 'My job change into management was completely unsupported – my requests for training took months, and by the time they were approved the need had passed. Yes, you learn on the job, but how much more constructive for all involved if it happens in a structured way. Surely this would speed up the learning curve?'

However, there are changes in the air. At Little Feet Publications, Barbara Foster has been overhauling the company's training and career structure so that all employees have regular appraisals. 'We are ahead of our competitors here at Little Feet, but even we are only beginning to scratch the surface. So far there's been little opposition to the appraisals, but there's still loads to do and the results will not become clear for a few years yet.'

Perhaps the industry should consider itself lucky to have so many dedicated managers who have, through a combination of chance and determination, successfully developed their careers in publishing. Clearly it now needs to review what is being done to develop, train and reward the next generation of bosses. Above all, the industry has to find more people with entrepreneurial spirit and push them into demanding roles rather than make them serve their time at a junior level. But such changes can only come from the very top.

Line 30

13 The writer says that in comparison to publishing, other companies

    A   are more concerned with pleasing their shareholders.
    B   are more focused on achieving their goals.
    C   place greater importance on keeping their best managers.
    D   work harder on interpersonal relationships.

14 Sarah Carter changed her job within William Davis Publishing because

    A   the Public Relations department made it clear they wanted her.
    B   she saw more long-term potential in public relations.
    C   she did not want to relocate to another floor.
    D   it represented a promotion for her.

15 Virginia Coutts says that when she first started at Prodigy Publications

    A   she intended to move on quickly.
    B   she had a wide range of skills.
    C   she had to do too many different jobs.
    D   she had a good line manager.

16 What does Mark Harlock say about formal training?

    A   It is faster than learning on the job.
    B   It should be based on the trainee's specific needs.
    C   It is more often approved for managers than other employees.
    D   It enables better working relationships to be built.

17 In using the words 'scratch the surface' (line 30), Barbara Foster means that her actions

    A   have started something that will take a lot of work to complete.
    B   have revealed big problems that she could not have foreseen.
    C   may turn out to be unpopular with some employees.
    D   may cause disputes with other publishers.

18 In the final paragraph, the writer recommends that the publishing industry should

    A   encourage managers to delegate minor matters more often.
    B   put pressure on directors to change the way they work.
    C   look for people with business flair and good ideas.
    D   spend more time training existing managers.

PART FOUR

Questions 19–33

- Read the article below about the UK retail sector.
- Choose the best word to fill each gap from **A**, **B**, **C** or **D** on the opposite page.
- For each question (**19–33**), mark one letter (**A**, **B**, **C** or **D**) on your Answer Sheet.
- There is an example at the beginning (**0**).

The Retail Sector

The retail sector is one of the UK's biggest employment areas, accounting for one in nine of the (**0**) .....B..... It is also one of the fastest growing – more than a fifth of jobs (**19**) .... last year were in retail. Such rapid (**20**) .... in the tightest labour market for more than a generation should be (**21**) .... up wages, but it is not. While the national (**22**) .... wage goes up by about 5% a year, in retail it goes up by 3.5%.

The consequences of low wages and far from brilliant conditions is rapid staff turnover. About half the staff employed in retail leave every year. This (**23**) .... is way above even those sectors such as nursing, which are said to be in a recruitment (**24**) .... Part of the problem is that the employers themselves are under considerable financial (**25**) .... Retail is suffering a long-term slide independent of the (**26**) .... and falls of the economy. One of the reasons for this is consumer expectations. With the growth of e-commerce, customers look for bigger and better bargains and insist on (**27**) .... for money.

There are some pluses for employees, however. Low wages and high turnover make retail a youthful sector. Real managerial (**28**) .... can be attained by the mid-20s, so school-leavers or recent graduates need only wait a short time before gaining promotion. And despite the problems, the retail sector does, on occasion, (**29**) .... some of the more progressive career (**30**) .... programmes. The supermarket chain Robertsons, for example, has a community service scheme that trains staff in team-building through work on neighbourhood projects. And clothes retailer P & R has an impressive (**31**) .... when it comes to employing older people. It pursues a (**32**) .... of employing mature people with long (**33**) .... of the products, as it believes they provide better customer service.

Example:

| A company | B workforce | C personnel | D organisation |

| 0 | A ☐ | B ▬ | C ☐ | D ☐ |

19	A made	B formed	C created	D appointed
20	A expansion	B increase	C addition	D extension
21	A getting	B pushing	C turning	D giving
22	A normal	B medium	C average	D common
23	A figure	B sum	C data	D calculation
24	A emergency	B disaster	C trouble	D crisis
25	A weight	B force	C power	D pressure
26	A climbs	B rises	C increases	D advances
27	A advantage	B benefit	C worth	D value
28	A care	B responsibility	C duty	D reliability
29	A cause	B present	C produce	D bring
30	A development	B outcome	C continuation	D progress
31	A report	B distinction	C credit	D record
32	A policy	B code	C procedure	D theory
33	A knowledge	B contact	C history	D experience

PART FIVE

Questions 34–45

- Read the book review below.
- In most of the lines (**34–45**), there is one extra word. It is either grammatically incorrect or does not fit in with the meaning of the text. Some lines, however, are correct.
- If a line is correct, write **CORRECT** on your Answer Sheet.
- If there is an extra word in the line, write the **extra word** in CAPITAL LETTERS on your Answer Sheet.
- The exercise begins with two examples (**0** and **00**).

Examples:	**0**	C	O	R	R	E	C	T		
	00	O	N							

Advertising for the Small Business by Nick Daws

0   Good communication with existing and potential customers is at the heart of

00 successful business. That is one reason why advertising should, and does, play on such

34 an important role in so many organisations itself. However, for the small business, unfamiliar

35 with or inexperienced at using advertising, the investment can seem uncertain. Unlike

36 to their counterparts in larger companies, with sizeable marketing departments and

37 professional advertising agencies, no managers in smaller firms often find themselves

38 facing a range of decisions about which campaign objectives and strategy, creative

39 content, budgets and media choice. The list goes on. That is why I was pleased about to read

40 Nick Daws' guide to the world of marketing communications. I use this phrase rather than

41 advertising because the book goes beyond of the weekly display advertisements in the local

42 paper. It also covers sales promotion, direct mail, point-of-sale and PR, all whose components of

43 the marketing mix that can be easily overlooked, but which are in fact resulting highly effective.

44 It also provides clear and comprehensive advice on the development of strategy, thus ensuring

45 that careful readers will succeed avoid the costly mistake of rushed or ill-considered decisions.

WRITING 45 minutes

PART ONE

- You have to change the date of a marketing meeting that was scheduled for next Friday.
- Write an **email** to all members of the marketing team:
  - giving the new date of the meeting
  - explaining why the date of the meeting has been changed
  - providing details of an additional point for the agenda.
- Write **40–50** words.

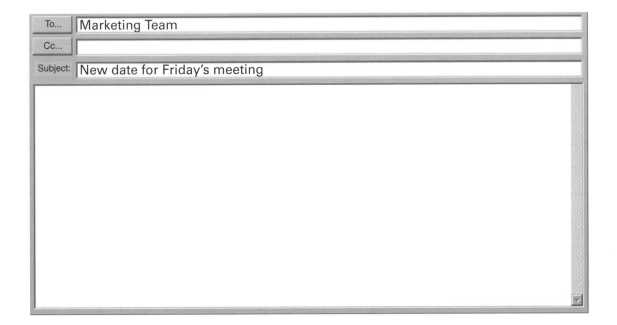

To...	Marketing Team
Cc...	
Subject:	New date for Friday's meeting

PART TWO

- The company you work for is developing a new product and needs to finance this. A group of investors called Venture Enterprises has sent you some information.
- Look at the information below, on which you have already made some handwritten notes.
- Then, using **all** your handwritten notes, write a **letter** to George Rodich.
- Write **120–140** words.

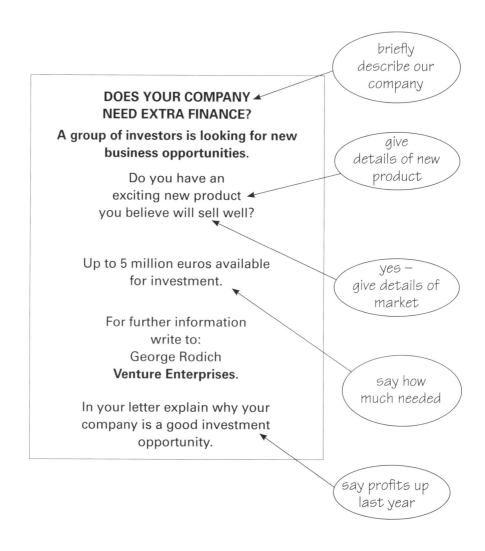

DOES YOUR COMPANY
NEED EXTRA FINANCE?

A group of investors is looking for new business opportunities.

Do you have an
exciting new product
you believe will sell well?

Up to 5 million euros available
for investment.

For further information
write to:
George Rodich
Venture Enterprises.

In your letter explain why your
company is a good investment
opportunity.

briefly describe our company

give details of new product

yes – give details of market

say how much needed

say profits up last year

LISTENING   40 minutes (including 10 minutes' transfer time)

PART ONE

Questions 1–12

- You will hear three telephone conversations or messages.
- Write **one or two words or a number** in the numbered spaces on the notes or forms below.
- After you have listened once, replay each recording.

Conversation One

(Questions 1–4)

- Look at the notes below.
- You will hear a woman giving information about a timetable.

INDUCTION PROGRAMME FOR NEW SALES STAFF

MONDAY   (1) ....

TUESDAY   *product development lab*

WEDNESDAY   *am* (2) .... *department*

                pm information about (3) ....

                in accounts dept.

THURSDAY   *meet the* (4) ....

Conversation Two

(Questions 5–8)

- Look at the note below.
- You will hear a woman leaving a message about some problems with her company's new product.

MESSAGE

To: *Jamie*

From: *Alice*

Re:

(5) .... *for Trimco HP4*

- *Problems have been discovered by the*

  (6) .... *staff.*

- *Can't proceed with* (7) ....

  as planned next month.

- *Alice travelling to Berlin to join*

  (8) ....

- *Will contact with new information ASAP.*

Conversation Three

(Questions 9–12)

- Look at the notes below.
- You will hear a manager telling a colleague about what happened in a meeting.

Website development meeting

Notes

Site most popular with **(9)** ....

Needs to be more attractive to **(10)** ....

Changes:

- include **(11)** ....
- add link to the **(12)** ....

PART TWO

Questions 13–22

Section One

(Questions 13–17)

- You will hear five short recordings about delivery problems.
- For each recording, decide which problem the speaker talks about.
- Write one letter (**A–H**) next to the number of the recording.
- Do not use any letter more than once.
- After you have listened once, replay the recordings.

13 ....

14 ....

15 ....

16 ....

17 ....

A	The goods were delivered late.
B	Goods were delivered without having been ordered.
C	The items ordered were unavailable.
D	Only part of our order was delivered.
E	The goods were damaged in transit.
F	Goods were packaged in the wrong quantities.
G	The sales literature about the goods was misleading.
H	Goods intended for one location were delivered to another.

Section Two

(Questions 18–22)

- You will hear another five recordings. Five people are talking about project management.
- For each recording, decide what action each speaker is recommending.
- Write one letter (**A–H**) next to the number of the recording.
- Do not use any letter more than once.
- After you have listened once, replay the recordings.

18 ....

19 ....

20 ....

21 ....

22 ....

A	defining objectives tightly
B	planning the schedule carefully
C	ensuring the plans have some flexibility
D	handing over some tasks to other team members
E	ensuring the team is motivated
F	dealing with problems promptly
G	arranging regular status meetings
H	keeping in constant email contact with team

PART THREE

Questions 23–30

- You will hear a radio interview with Donald White, the author of a book about running board meetings.
- For each question (**23–30**), mark one letter (**A**, **B** or **C**) for the correct answer.
- After you have listened once, replay the recording.

23   According to White, what do most people think happens at board meetings?

    A   Participants discuss the company's future in a creative way.
    B   Participants tell each other how successful the company is.
    C   Participants compete with each other to gain more power.

24   What does White think is the key to having a successful board meeting?

    A   inviting the right people to the meeting
    B   choosing a chair who handles the paperwork efficiently
    C   ensuring people are able to prepare for the meeting

25   According to White, what should report presenters do at board meetings?

    A   present a summary of their report
    B   focus on conclusions of their report
    C   answer questions about their report

26   What kind of person does White think makes the best chairs?

    A   a person who previously held the office of chief executive
    B   an experienced person who may be a future chief executive
    C   an inexperienced person who is keen to learn new skills

27   What does White say the chair has to be able to do?

    A   ensure that decisions are reached quickly
    B   draw attention to the weaknesses in any argument
    C   give all points of view the chance to be expressed

28   How does White feel about how agendas are prepared?

    A   irritated that so much time is spent discussing them
    B   concerned that they are prepared by senior staff
    C   surprised that so little thought is given to them

29   What suggestion does White make about the agenda?

   A   The content of the agenda should be considered on a yearly basis.
   B   Routine matters should not always be at the top of the agenda.
   C   Time limits should be imposed on discussions of less important issues.

30   What does White recommend about what happens after the meeting?

   A   Action points from the meeting must be dealt with promptly.
   B   The record of the meeting must be very carefully checked.
   C   Someone must report back on the meeting to anyone who could not attend.

You now have 10 minutes to transfer your answers to your Answer Sheet.

SPEAKING   14 minutes

SAMPLE SPEAKING TASKS

PART ONE

In this part, the interlocutor asks questions to each of the candidates in turn. You have to give information about yourself and express personal opinions.

PART TWO

In this part of the test, you are asked to give a short talk on a business topic. You have to choose one of the topics from the three below and then talk for about one minute. You have one minute to prepare your ideas.

A: **What is important when . . . ?**

Designing a reception area
- Company image
- Security
-
-

B: **What is important when . . . ?**

Organising a conference
- Conference speakers
- Facilities at conference centre
-
-

C: **What is important when . . . ?**

Setting a budget for developing a product
- Predicted sales
- Quality of product
-
-

PART THREE

In this part of the test, you are given a discussion topic. You have 30 seconds to look at the task prompt, an example of which is below, and then about three minutes to discuss the topic with your partner. After that, the examiner will ask you more questions related to the topic.

For **two** candidates

Travel Costs

The company you work for wants to reduce the amount it spends on business trips abroad.

You have been asked to suggest ways of doing this.

Discuss the situation together and decide:

- how the total number of business trips might be reduced
- how the cost of some trips might be reduced.

For **three** candidates

Travel Costs

The company you work for wants to reduce the amount it spends on business trips abroad.

You have been asked to suggest ways of doing this.

Discuss the situation together and decide:

- how the total number of business trips might be reduced
- how the cost of some trips might be reduced
- how to make business trips more productive.

Follow-on questions

- Do you think it causes problems for companies when managers are frequently away on business? (Why?/Why not?)

- Would you enjoy travelling overseas on business? (Why?/Why not?)

- Do you think most managers enjoy travelling overseas on business? (Why?/Why not?)

- Do you think a reduction in business travel could make a company less competitive? (Why?/Why not?)

- Should managers be allowed to take their family with them on business trips? (Why?/Why not?)

Test 3

READING   1 hour

PART ONE

Questions 1–7

- Look at the statements below and the extract on the opposite page from a report to staff by the Davis Group, a human resources consultancy in the USA.
- Which section (**A, B, C** or **D**) does each statement (**1–7**) refer to?
- For each statement (**1–7**), mark one letter (**A, B, C** or **D**) on your Answer Sheet.
- You will need to use some of these letters more than once.

Example:

0   It is less expensive to maintain the current customer base than to increase it.

---

1   The company has had limited success in convincing customers that it can offer a variety of human resources solutions.

2   It has been necessary to monitor expenditure carefully.

3   Expertise in different cultures is a major selling point for the company.

4   The company's performance is strongly linked to its reputation.

5   The company is confident of its ability to expand.

6   The company makes ongoing efforts to improve the standard of its service provision.

7   Many consulting businesses have performed badly in this period.

Report for Staff

A   It has been a challenging year, with the global economy contributing to increased market competition. However, the end results were fairly respectable, especially considering the industry's generally poor financial results. The Davis Group has always focused on growing revenue, solving client problems, identifying new opportunities and winning new clients. Although the company had to spend more time than usual this year on cost control, our people continued to listen to their clients and deliver appropriate consulting solutions.

B   Although we have changed our name and introduced a new global brand, many clients still do not regard us as a broad-based human resources consultancy. We hope that our new international campaign, which explains to clients the wide range of services we offer, will help change that perception. It is significant that 50% of our revenue this year came from outside the USA, making us a truly global player. We have enormous growth potential, especially in emerging markets such as Asia and Latin America.

C   These days, most of our clients, even those with operations in only one country, compete in a global marketplace. As a result, they see the value of working with us. Our strength on the ground in many countries has allowed us to share knowledge to develop and deliver world-class solutions. For those clients who are global firms, our worldwide presence has allowed us to build international networks to address their special needs. They appreciate that our intellectual capital is based on a deep understanding of local needs and conditions.

D   We continually aim to maximise our revenue and enhance professionalism across the solutions offered by the firm. Obviously, winning new clients is always important, but we should remember that it is often easier and more cost-effective to broaden relationships with existing clients. By providing a wider range of solutions, we add value, strengthen our clients' view of us as a trusted advisor and build long-term partnerships. Our success is based on being known as the most professional and highest quality firm in the human resources consultancy business.

PART TWO

Questions 8–12

- Read the article below about the differences between chief executives and entrepreneurs.
- Choose the best sentence from the opposite page to fill each of the gaps.
- For each gap (**8–12**), mark one letter (**A–G**) on your Answer Sheet.
- Do not use any letter more than once.
- There is an example at the beginning (**0**).

Analysing the Entrepreneur

The ever-increasing attraction of under-graduate courses in business studies demonstrates that many young people begin their working lives determined to be a success in business. Many of them will have ambitions of becoming bosses. (**0**) ..... G ..... That should be the question which all ambitious young business people ask themselves.

Some graduates learn how to run a business in someone else's time, and then in their early thirties, start out on their own. That course of action is relatively common and straightforward. (**8**) .... Often, however, their business flair comes at the expense of more mundane business skills such as team building and maintaining harmony.

A recent study, in which seventeen successful entrepreneurs took part in in-depth interviews, as did a similar number of chief executives, concluded that honesty and strong moral principles are important characteristics of entrepreneurs who achieve lasting success. According to the various tests and self-assessment questionnaires used in the interviews, seventy per cent of entrepreneurs have these characteristics, as opposed to only twenty-eight per cent of chief executives. (**9**) .... It would seem that most entrepreneurs deserve more credit than people generally give them.

This ethical style of leadership fosters a culture in which expectations are uncompromisingly high and in which people believe they will be properly rewarded for their individual contribution. (**10**) .... Employees often complain that the worst kind of bosses are the ones who own the business, as they can be very intolerant of others who make mistakes.

Entrepreneurs are passionate about their work but they have not worked their way up through the organisation and tend to lack the people management qualities that chief executives have developed over long careers. (**11**) .... Of course, it could be argued that the single-minded approach of entrepreneurs is what makes them successful; it certainly enables them to put extraordinary effort into what they do.

The study indicates that generally chief executives can match entrepreneurs in terms of drive and determination. There is one exception and that relates to taking risks. (**12**) .... The chief executive can, on the other hand, always move to another company.

But in the end, if there are no entrepreneurs, there is no work for chief executives. It is the people that start businesses who are the original wealth creators.

Example:

A However, it can also result in entrepreneurs being profoundly disappointed when others fail to live up to their high standards.

B They need to have the confidence to make everyone in the organisation believe that this is no ordinary place and no ordinary job.

C Given the common perception that entrepreneurs are only in business to make money, this very positive finding was perhaps the most surprising.

D They are less likely to promote teamwork and co-operation than chief executives, who are much better at reading and understanding those around them.

E After all, if it is your own company, you cannot walk away, and you will do anything either to keep it afloat or to help it prosper.

F But true entrepreneurs do not necessarily wait until their business knowledge has improved or until the time is right – they have always been driven to achieve.

G But is it best for them to become entrepreneurs and start their own business or work towards running someone else's?

PART THREE

Questions 13–18

- Read the magazine article below about Andy Seymour, the Chief Executive of a chain of book stores called Bookroom, and the questions on the opposite page.
- For each question (**13–18**), mark one letter (**A**, **B**, **C** or **D**) on your Answer Sheet.

CHALLENGING TIMES AT BOOKROOM

Bookroom isn't a very successful company at the moment. It's heavily in debt, and it's rumoured that its owner, P&K, wouldn't turn down a suitable offer. Even its own store managers are said to be unhappy – those who haven't left, that is. A recent change in strategy is proving too much for many of them: they've been told to concentrate on giving more space to a limited number of bestsellers, advertised nationally by the company, and not to titles which sit on the shelves for weeks.

The challenge of taking Bookroom back into profit falls to the Chief Executive, Andy Seymour, who was moved a year ago from P&K's music chain, MusicWorld, with an impressive record of efficiency improvements. He increased the floor space of the more successful MusicWorld stores and closed down the loss-making ones. New computer systems gave him better stock control, and allowed him to produce up-to-date charts of the top CDs for display in the stores, with a positive impact on turnover and profits. In addition, he negotiated a pay and productivity deal with the employees. All in all, it was a period which saw the chain reach its peak.

Seymour, though, doesn't take any credit for MusicWorld's success. 'Even before I became Chief Executive, all the stores were run by top quality people doing everything they could, at a time when the public weren't spending much on leisure,' he says. 'They all stayed on, and that was the decisive factor. The only things I did were to change the advertising agency – they weren't keeping up with developments in the music industry – and make some minor innovations in the stores. Customers were coming into the shops, and it was up to us to make the most of this.'

Luck had been against him in his previous job, though, as operations director of Clarkson's, the do-it-yourself retailer which P&K had just acquired. Soon after his move to the company, there was a recession, which meant that the market for home improvement products collapsed. Seymour was involved in endless consultations with the board, discussing ways to turn the company round. They were in a high-risk situation and, despite his efforts, Clarkson's lost millions. But even when things were at their worst, Seymour didn't resign, as most would have done, and he was highly thought of for that.

He has a reasonable track record, certainly, but some would say not brilliant. And will he succeed at Bookroom? His first year has been disappointing, but there are signs of improvement. He's continued the strategy of opening new shops, and although many store managers have gone, their replacements have been picked carefully. He's also done something about one of the main reasons for the present difficulties, reducing targets to allow for the fact that the book market is still flat.

Seymour is an experienced retail manager. At MusicWorld he proved himself a good manager of people with a particular gift for motivating his staff. But he's also strong on detail, and has already improved Bookroom's financial control. It looks as though his strategy will pay off in the long term. The only thing you could blame him for is not being strong enough in opposing all the negative talk about Bookroom, because that is what is damaging the company. And unless Seymour does something about that, he may find himself looking for a new job.

13 According to the first paragraph, what are Bookroom store managers not pleased about?

- **A** the number of recent staff redundancies
- **B** the reduction in the range of books on sale
- **C** P&K's current plans to sell the company
- **D** P&K's approach towards advertising different titles

14 Which of the following contributed to Andy Seymour's success at MusicWorld?

- **A** investing more time in researching music trends
- **B** training staff to use the computerised order system
- **C** offering staff a greater incentive to sell more items
- **D** bringing new stock into the poorly performing stores

15 Seymour says that MusicWorld was successful because

- **A** sales of music products were booming.
- **B** the store managers were very capable.
- **C** its advertising had been highly effective.
- **D** his innovations attracted a wider target group.

16 While Seymour worked for Clarkson's he was respected because he

- **A** was willing to take certain risks in order to stay in business.
- **B** had predicted the downturn in the home improvements industry.
- **C** kept the store managers informed about the company's situation.
- **D** continued as director despite the company experiencing difficulties.

17 According to the writer, Bookroom had problems during Seymour's first year because

- **A** he had been too cautious about the location of new stores.
- **B** he failed to recognise what consumers were looking for.
- **C** there was a shortage of suitable staff to take over managers' jobs.
- **D** the expected volume of book sales had been unrealistic.

18 In the last paragraph, the writer suggests that in his present role, Seymour needs to

- **A** take action to improve the company's reputation.
- **B** pay more attention to every aspect of his strategy.
- **C** make sure there are sufficient funds for his expansion plans.
- **D** encourage loyalty by strengthening staff-management relationships.

PART FOUR

Questions 19–33

- Read the article below about goods returned by customers to mail order companies.
- Choose the best word or phrase to fill each gap from **A**, **B**, **C** or **D** on the opposite page.
- For each question (**19–33**), mark one letter (**A**, **B**, **C** or **D**) on your Answer Sheet.
- There is an example at the beginning (**0**).

Unwanted Goods

Increased sales is always good news for mail order companies. But more sales also (**0**) ....A..... more items are returned. Most companies have a full returns policy, but as Meg Powell, Managing Director of mail order company Go First, explains, this usually (**19**) .... a lot of extra work. 'If an item comes back, we have to (**20**) .... with refunds, apology mailings and stock control. This is a complex process and each returned item undergoes close (**21**) .... for defects. If goods are in a fit (**22**) .... for stock, they need repacking and putting back in the warehouse. If not, we'll look at why. Anything (**23**) .... to the quality of returned goods is (**24**) .... information. In some instances we can identify a fault in production and do something about it.'

Estimates of the number of returns for the sector (**25**) .... In the (**26**) .... of Go First, which delivers 100 million packages a year, 26 million come back. Reducing this number is an important (**27**) .... for the company. One way it aims to do this is by making the initial order-taking process as accurate as possible, and by closely (**28**) .... the packing of goods. (**29**) .... the reasons for returns also helps. Go First telephones a (**30**) .... of people returning goods to establish their reasons for doing so.

Clearly, a customer-focused returns process is essential for fostering trust in the company. 'It is standard (**31**) .... in this business,' says Meg Powell. 'It attracts customers, gives them a greater (**32**) .... of security and encourages them to buy. We realise that making the return of goods a smooth, fast process can only (**33**) .... customer satisfaction.'

Example:

   A means   **B** leads   **C** proposes   **D** gives

0	A B C D
	▄ ▭ ▭ ▭

19	**A** contains	**B** includes	**C** concerns	**D** involves
20	**A** handle	**B** deal	**C** treat	**D** manage
21	**A** attention	**B** inquiry	**C** inspection	**D** survey
22	**A** condition	**B** situation	**C** form	**D** arrangement
23	**A** combining	**B** affecting	**C** influencing	**D** relating
24	**A** key	**B** main	**C** central	**D** major
25	**A** alter	**B** move	**C** disagree	**D** vary
26	**A** place	**B** state	**C** case	**D** position
27	**A** objective	**B** purpose	**C** direction	**D** scheme
28	**A** estimating	**B** monitoring	**C** researching	**D** measuring
29	**A** Carrying out	**B** Looking into	**C** Getting in	**D** Seeing to
30	**A** choice	**B** preference	**C** selection	**D** pick
31	**A** system	**B** practice	**C** operation	**D** method
32	**A** perception	**B** sense	**C** belief	**D** instinct
33	**A** boost	**B** expand	**C** push	**D** enlarge

PART FIVE

Questions 34–45

- Read the text below about information technology (IT) training.
- In most of the lines (**34–45**), there is one extra word. It is either grammatically incorrect or does not fit in with the meaning of the text. Some lines, however, are correct.
- If the line is correct, write **CORRECT**, on your Answer Sheet.
- If there is an extra word in the line, write **the extra word** in CAPITAL LETTERS on your Answer Sheet.
- The exercise begins with two examples (**0** and **00**).

Examples:	**0**	S	U	C	H				
	00	C	O	R	R	E	C	T	

IT Training

0 The arrival of a sophisticated computer system is a such big event in any

00 organisation, but it is obviously difficult to make the most of this type of investment

34 without proper training. IT training can be expensive cost and, despite the good

35 intentions of the people are involved, a huge amount of training is wasted every year.

36 Quite frequently, until staff continue to struggle with computer systems that either

37 they do not understand, or they can only exploit to a fraction of their true

38 potential. A common mistake is made to rush in and train people too soon. This is

39 to be expected. Quite reasonably, the logic is so that it is better to train people early

40 than not to do it at all. The difficulty, however, is that people's memories are short, so it is

41 better to train people when the 'go live' date which is known. This way their knowledge

42 will still be fresh when they have to put it into practice. It may also be an error

43 to commission an external training organisation because of their standard materials

44 may not be suitable. An alternative one is to pilot the software with a team of capable

45 employees and once again they are familiar with its operation, they can then train

other staff.

WRITING 45 minutes

PART ONE

- You work in the Information Technology department of a large company.
  There has been a delay setting up a new computer system.
- Write an **email** to all staff:
  - apologising for the delay
  - explaining why there was a problem setting up the new system
  - saying when the new system will be ready.
- Write **40–50** words.

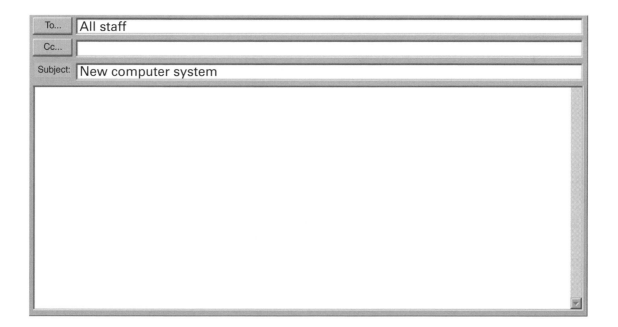

To...	All staff
Cc...	
Subject:	New computer system

PART TWO

- You work in the sales department of a large television manufacturer. Your line manager at head office has asked you for a report about sales in your region.
- Look at the information below, on which you have already made some handwritten notes.
- Then, using **all** your handwritten notes, write your **report**.
- Write **120–140** words.

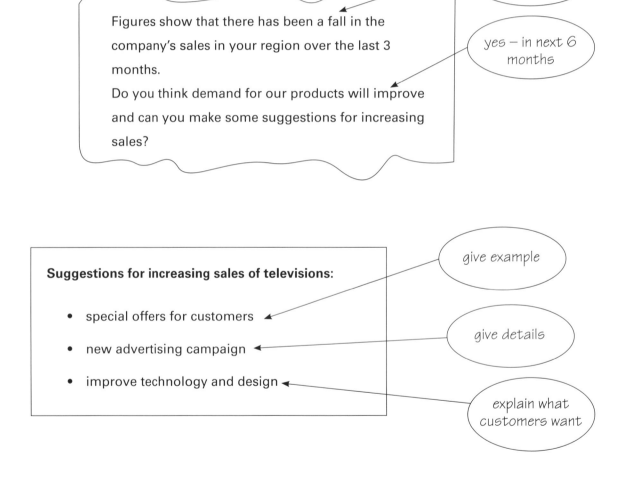

all retail sales fallen!

Figures show that there has been a fall in the company's sales in your region over the last 3 months.

Do you think demand for our products will improve and can you make some suggestions for increasing sales?

yes – in next 6 months

Suggestions for increasing sales of televisions:

- special offers for customers
- new advertising campaign
- improve technology and design

give example

give details

explain what customers want

LISTENING 40 minutes (including 10 minutes' transfer time)

PART ONE

Questions 1–12

- You will hear three telephone conversations or messages.
- Write **one or two words or a number** in the numbered spaces on the notes or forms below.
- After you have listened once, replay each recording.

Conversation One

(Questions 1–4)

- Look at the note below.
- You will hear a man calling a colleague about making changes to his schedule.

JACKSON'S ASSOCIATES
Telephone Message

Caller: James Horrocks

Date and time of call: 6th April 9.45 am

Message

RESCHEDULE MORNING:

The meeting with John Row (APF) will need to be **(1)** ....

The new time of the marketing meeting is: **(2)** ....

Call Jim Davis to arrange a **(3)** ....

Also, send **(4)** .... to Freda Bell.

Conversation Two

(Questions 5–8)

- Look at the notes below.
- You will hear a woman leaving a message for a colleague about his slides for a presentation.

Christine's comments on slides

- Remove the (**5**) .... and put in some words.

- The (**6**) .... of the slides needs to be improved.

- The (**7**) .... on slide 3 doesn't make sense.

- There's a (**8**) .... on slide 6.

Conversation Three

(Questions 9–12)

- Look at the notes below.
- You will hear a woman giving instructions to a colleague about dealing with job applications.

Applications for Publicity Co-ordinator

Things to do:

- Reject those without

  (9) .... qualifications.

- Select those who've done work in a

  (10) ....

- Request (11) .... for people on shortlist.

- Circulate applications to (12) ....

PART TWO

Questions 13–22

Section One

(Questions 13–17)

- You will hear five short recordings. Five people are giving advice on how to give feedback to employees.
- For each recording, decide what advice the speaker gives.
- Write one letter (**A–H**) next to the number of the recording.
- Do not use any letter more than once.
- After you have listened once, replay the recordings.

13	**A**	Give feedback on a regular basis.
	B	Choose the right time and place.
14	**C**	Focus on the consequences of the individual's behaviour.
15	**D**	Ignore your own personal feelings.
	E	Be clear about what you're referring to.
16	**F**	Praise the individual's strengths.
	G	Offer people the chance to respond.
17	**H**	Give feedback immediately.

Section Two

(Questions 18–22)

- You will hear another five recordings. Five people are talking about their reasons for joining a particular company.
- For each recording, decide why the speaker chose to join the company.
- Write one letter (**A–H**) next to the number of the recording.
- Do not use any letter more than once.
- After you have listened once, replay the recordings.

18	**A**	It was close to home.
	B	The interview process was friendly.
19	**C**	The workload was not too demanding.
	D	There was a wide variety of work on offer.
20	**E**	The financial benefits were attractive.
	F	The management approach was dynamic.
21	**G**	There were relevant training opportunities.
	H	The promotion prospects were good.
22		

PART THREE

Questions 23–30

- You will hear the Chief Executive of Best Value, an American chain of convenience stores, talking about a change in the company's working practices.
- For each question (**23–30**), mark one letter (**A**, **B** or **C**) for the correct answer.
- After you have listened once, replay the recording.

23   When the speaker became Chief Executive of Best Value, most employees

    A   were given little information about the company.
    B   had no input into the decision-making process.
    C   felt a lack of commitment to the company.

24   Best Value introduced Performance Management in order to

    A   increase the employees' job satisfaction.
    B   speed up the expansion of the workforce.
    C   improve pay and conditions for its staff.

25   Why did Best Value decide to introduce Performance Management into its distribution centres first?

    A   It would be less complicated to work with a small number of sites.
    B   Improving the distribution centres would also benefit the stores.
    C   The distribution centres' problems were easier to solve than those of the stores.

26   When introducing Performance Management, Best Value made a list of

    A   positions that needed a change in responsibilities.
    B   staff who needed to be given new positions.
    C   the skills required for each position.

27   The speaker believes the main reason why Performance Management is effective is

    A   the ease with which staff can reach targets.
    B   the efficiency of the new work systems.
    C   the attention that staff receive.

28   Compared with the company's other distribution centres, what was surprising about the new one in California?

    A   It was the only one providing training for all staff.
    B   It had the lowest level of absenteeism.
    C   It required fewer staff than the others.

29 What is unusual about the new distribution centre in Texas?

    A   the accuracy of its deliveries

    B   the number of supervisors it employs

    C   the high level of sales in the stores it services

30 In the speaker's opinion, what is the greatest benefit of Performance Management?

    A   It allows more demanding objectives to be set.

    B   It makes positive behaviour into a habit.

    C   It leads to a significant reduction in costs.

You now have 10 minutes to transfer your answers to your Answer Sheet.

SPEAKING   14 minutes

SAMPLE SPEAKING TASKS

PART ONE

In this part, the interlocutor asks questions to each of the candidates in turn. You have to give information about yourself and express personal opinions.

PART TWO

In this part of the test, you are asked to give a short talk on a business topic. You have to choose one of the topics from the three below and then talk for about one minute. You have one minute to prepare your ideas.

A: What is important when . . . ?

Trying to attract new staff
- Competitive wages
- Company reputation
-
-

B: What is important when . . . ?

Delegating work to others
- Clear instructions
- Choice of person for the task
-
-

C: What is important when . . . ?

Designing a company website
- Type of information to include
- Different language versions
-
-

PART THREE

In this part of the test, you are given a discussion topic. You have 30 seconds to look at the task prompt, an example of which is below, and then about three minutes to discuss the topic with your partner. After that, the examiner will ask you more questions related to the topic.

For **two** candidates

Sales Managers Conference

Your company is organising a conference for the sales managers working in its offices around the world.

You have been asked to help plan the conference.

Discuss the situation together and decide:

- what information you will need to send to the sales managers before the conference

- what activities you could organise to help people to get to know each other better.

For **three** candidates

Sales Managers Conference

Your company is organising a conference for the sales managers working in its offices around the world.

You have been asked to help plan the conference.

Discuss the situation together and decide:

- what information you will need to send to the sales managers before the conference

- what activities you could organise to help people to get to know each other better

- what facilities you will provide at the conference.

Follow-on questions

- Do you think a company benefits from holding conferences for its employees? (Why?/Why not?)

- Do you think you would enjoy going to a conference? (Why?/Why not?)

- How important is location to the success of a conference? (Why?/Why not?)

- Could it be a problem if several managers in a company are away at conferences at the same time? (Why?/Why not?)

- Apart from having conferences, what other ways can companies encourage teamwork among their employees?

Test 4

READING   1 hour

PART ONE

Questions 1–7

- Look at the statements below and the article about meetings on the opposite page.
- Which section (**A, B, C** or **D**) does each statement (**1–7**) refer to?
- For each statement (**1–7**), mark one letter (**A, B, C** or **D**) on your Answer Sheet.
- You will need to use some of these letters more than once.

Example:

0   a policy of not allowing people in meetings to become comfortable and relaxed

---

1   a way of ensuring that meetings are less likely to take place

2   the common situation of too many people attending meetings

3   a way of ensuring communication can take place without breaking company rules

4   a policy discouraging repetition of ideas

5   staff attitudes towards meetings resulting in action to reduce their frequency

6   a policy of cutting down on the amount of detail given in long speeches

7   people who attend meetings requesting limitations on other forms of communication

Business Meetings

A   Many organisations are developing ways of minimising the time workers spend sitting in meetings in order to give them more hours working at their desks. They realise that reducing the number of meetings is problematic, but some are using a device called a Meeting Meter to determine how much money is wasted through the widespread practice of over-populated and time-inefficient meetings. A general meeting in a big company can cost £9000 an hour. Even staff in UK government departments have been told to make less elaborate presentations and to get through them more quickly.

B   A solution has often been to take things at breakneck speed or abolish meetings altogether. Olivia Dacourt, CEO of a retail chain, makes a point of not letting anyone sit down in her meetings. 'We cover more material in a 15-minute meeting than you'd see in a two-hour sit-down meeting,' she says. She drills her employees to shout 'pass' if they have no comment to make, thereby saving a hastily mumbled agreement with the previous speaker. In this way, her last staff meeting clocked in at six minutes.

C   Website designer Barry Hare has gone so far as to charge his clients a meeting 'tax'. If they ask for a meeting, he doubles his design fee of £85 an hour. 'Everyone I talk to hates meetings, but they don't know what to do about them,' he says. 'Well, I've actually done something.' Similarly, at JP Products, managers have instigated a No Meetings Day every Friday. The scheme was devised by in-house industrial psychologist Ada Pearson after hearing employees joke about the need for a 'meeting-free day'.

D   But abolishing meetings is not as simple as clearing them from your diary. At JP Products some workers have felt the need to get round the No Meetings Day directive by holding spontaneous 'huddles' and 'nice to knows' to update each other on progress. After her success in reducing the meetings quota, Pearson is under pressure from meeting-weary managers to implement days that are free of emails and telephone calls. But unfortunately she has other priorities – thanks to a lengthy meeting with the chief executive.

PART TWO

Questions 8–12

- Read the article below about professional headhunters.
- Choose the best sentence from the opposite page to fill each of the gaps.
- For each gap (**8–12**), mark one letter (**A–G**) on your Answer Sheet.
- Do not use any letter more than once.
- There is an example at the beginning (**0**).

Attracting the headhunters

Professional headhunters are now key players in many kinds of recruitment.
But how do you gain their attention? Matthew Lynn investigates.

In the past, companies would use the services of headhunters to recruit principally at boardroom level. But these days, they are also responsible for filling a much wider range of middle management and specialist posts, and consequently, they have huge influence in the commercial world.

(**0**) .....G...... The first is that economic expansion has, in many countries, left the labour market tight. In a number of industries, and in growth sectors such as technology and media, there is now a severe shortage of skilled and talented people. This has forced companies to go out and look for the staff they need and not wait for them to arrive at the door. The second reason is that companies are now critically dependent on the skills and knowledge of their key people. They are very aware that having the right staff may determine their survival in a competitive marketplace. (**8**) ....

So, how do you make sure you get noticed by the headhunters? In the days when jobs were mainly advertised in newspapers, you could search the appointment pages and apply for anything that interested you. (**9**) .... Unless you are in contact with them, it is unlikely you will even be considered for a post.

Most headhunters will devote time and energy to tracking down talented people in large organisations. (**10**).............. So, while it would be nice to think the headhunters will find you, in fact, you often have to find them. 'Executives must be proactive in the search process by building on current skills, being fully prepared for interviews and by keeping CVs up to date,' says Julia Fernandez, manager of PB Executive Search.

It is also important that you set time aside to talk to headhunters. At some point, you may be contacted by a headhunter to recommend someone in a related field or provide a reference for someone you have dealt with professionally. If you simply deal with the enquiry as quickly as possible, you may be failing to exploit the potential benefit to yourself. (**11**) .... Fernandez advises that, 'All contact with headhunters is potentially useful, and you should have one or two headhunters that you know personally and make a point of keeping in touch with. (**12**) .... Make sure that the people around you will always be motivated to say something positive about you if approached. Your potential employers are watching you constantly.'

Example: 0 |

A But it is hard for them to establish contact unless these skilled individuals have been brought to their attention.

B They are consequently a lot more willing to turn to headhunters than in the past.

C Moreover, headhunters are all in the business of having as big a network as possible and working it to their advantage.

D In addition, the fact that headhunters are always looking for talent means that great care needs to be taken with the image you project in the workplace.

E Now, it is only junior or unskilled jobs that are filled this way; most of the best jobs are filled by headhunters.

F Not making the most of such an approach would definitely be a mistake.

G There are two reasons for this growing use of headhunters.

PART THREE

Questions 13–18

- Read the article below about Marc Hooper, CEO of the confectionery group Spartan Ketley, and the questions on the opposite page.
- For each question (**13–18**), mark one letter (**A**, **B**, **C** or **D**) on your Answer Sheet.

Marc Hooper, CEO of Spartan Ketley

Marc Hooper, not long promoted to CEO of confectionery giant Spartan Ketley (SK), is very different from his predecessors. He is a corporate lawyer by training, and his background has clearly shaped his management style. He was taught that no work should go unchecked and that no statement can go out without everything being fully defined. 'The legal world teaches you to think in a synthetic way, to take contrasting ideas and thread them together to form a strategy.' Hooper, with little marketing experience, was not at the top of market observers' lists for the job. But here he is, just over a year into the role and seemingly on top of things.

Educated at Harvard University, Hooper started his career with well-known New York consultants Cox & Leight (C&L), and became a specialist in mergers and acquisitions. 'It was a tremendous training ground and I could have stayed in mergers and acquisitions – I found the work interesting.' But another opportunity presented itself: SK offered him a job as general advisor. Hooper knew SK well because C&L was its main New York consultancy firm and Hooper looked after its account.

Hooper liked SK and when they came calling, several factors weighed on his mind. 'I admired SK and thought it would be a great place to work. C&L had told me I was only five years through a ten-year journey to become a partner. Also, for three years in a row my pay at C&L had stayed the same. Finally, I was working very long hours in a large, impersonal office and it seemed like an intelligent lifestyle decision to take a job with a different company.'

Hooper became established at SK, and soon felt ready for a higher position, but was told that no one could get on at SK unless they had been in sales and marketing. 'I had to make a move,' says Hooper. 'I took a risk; I became head of marketing in Europe.' In fact this was a sideways move – not for more money but to add to his knowledge and to further his career. The first challenge was that he found himself in charge of 25 bright young marketing people. 'I had to work hard to keep up,' he admits.

Throughout, he has remained focused, his eye always on the main prize. His elevation to CEO, he says, is proof of SK's inclusiveness. 'We are always open to people with fresh ideas. As CEO I support anyone who is willing to take a chance and who wants to stretch themselves. If you are keen to develop and prove you can succeed, this company will provide the challenge you need.' And in line with this philosophy, Hooper is not an autocratic leader: his style is to consult, to seek advice, then to act.

SK has grown quickly, mostly by acquisition. Hooper sits at the head of an empire that employs 50,000 people in 130 factories. His chief mission is to reduce waste in the company, to bring down costs, and to produce funds to reinvest – all the time keeping ahead of competitors. 'We must generate growth on a consistent basis. We've also got to generate more cash for investment in marketing.' The latest development, the purchase of a chocolate manufacturer for $42 billion – a deal managed by Hooper – has made it one of the largest confectionery groups in the world.

13   The choice of Marc Hooper as Spartan Ketley's CEO was surprising because

   A   he knew more about law than marketing.
   B   he had little experience of strategic planning.
   C   he had been with the company for a short time.
   D   he intended to take the company in a different direction.

14   What does Hooper say about his first job?

   A   He regarded the job as a means to a more interesting career.
   B   He gained useful skills while he was with the company.
   C   He found that his education prepared him well for the job.
   D   He enjoyed working for such a prestigious company.

15   One of the reasons for Hooper leaving Cox and Leight was

   A   he had no chance of becoming a partner.
   B   he was not happy with the working conditions.
   C   he wanted to move to a workplace in a different area.
   D   he felt it was important to change jobs every few years.

16   After some time at Spartan Ketley, Hooper changed departments because

   A   he did not find his current job financially rewarding enough.
   B   he wanted to have experience of working in Europe.
   C   it was an opportunity to work with young people.
   D   it improved his chances of promotion.

17   Hooper says that his policy as CEO is to

   A   develop a sense of competition within his workforce.
   B   train people to become proficient in a wide range of skills.
   C   hire staff who are not afraid to make important decisions.
   D   encourage employees to be innovative in their approach to work.

18   What does Hooper see as his main future task as CEO of Spartan Ketley?

   A   to bring greater diversity to the marketing of new products
   B   to increase the size of the company by acquiring a competitor
   C   to facilitate investment by improving the company's efficiency
   D   to investigate the possibility of diversifying into other manufacturing sectors

PART FOUR

Questions 19–33

- Read the article below about a company that sells household products.
- Choose the best word to fill each gap from **A**, **B**, **C** or **D** on the opposite page.
- For each question (**19–33**), mark one letter (**A**, **B**, **C** or **D**) on your Answer Sheet.
- There is an example at the beginning (**0**).

DAC's Margins Hit in Battle of the Brands

In a surprise trading statement, DAC Household Products yesterday gave (**0**) .....C..... of lower margins and weak profits growth. Shares in the company slumped by 22p to 459p after DAC said that its forecast of double-digit earnings growth in 2009 had been (**19**) .... to low single digits. The company (**20**) .... that it had failed to spend enough on promoting its own brands and conceded that its market share in India was under assault from (**21**) .... discounting by various competitors. Its major rival, KC Products, is offering big price discounts to attract consumers from DAC brands, which have traditionally (**22**) .... the household products sector. DAC also predicted a downturn in consumer (**23**) .... and strong price competition in Europe, and signalled that it was making (**24**) .... for an expensive brands battle.

DAC's chairman, David Chan, said that sales volumes had behaved as predicted, but that waves of discounting and store promotions from rivals had adversely (**25**) .... price forecasts. As a (**26**) .... the company now needed to increase investment in advertising and introduce keener pricing.

DAC had until (**27**) .... sought to increase revenue growth at the same time as improving profit margins. However, Chan confirmed that margins would be (**28**) .... as DAC increased spending on advertising and promotion to (**29**) .... those products under attack from competing brands. 'This commitment means (**30**) .... the long-term health of the business ahead of the (**31**) .... of short-term financial targets,' he said.

Rudy Mitcham, DAC's finance director, said that the company's recent cost-cutting programme would be (**32**) .... to help finance the increased spending, although he declined to reveal the (**33**) .... amount of money it would invest in additional advertising and promotion.

Example:

A advice	**B** caution	**C** warning	**D** threat

0	**A** ☐ **B** ☐ **C** ■ **D** ☐

19	**A** diminished	**B** fallen	**C** declined	**D** reduced
20	**A** admitted	**B** expressed	**C** communicated	**D** confided
21	**A** stern	**B** heavy	**C** harsh	**D** stiff
22	**A** directed	**B** governed	**C** dominated	**D** ruled
23	**A** assurance	**B** confidence	**C** belief	**D** conviction
24	**A** actions	**B** measures	**C** preparations	**D** steps
25	**A** touched	**B** affected	**C** changed	**D** impacted
26	**A** conclusion	**B** result	**C** reaction	**D** development
27	**A** presently	**B** formerly	**C** previously	**D** recently
28	**A** sacrificed	**B** ruined	**C** surrendered	**D** destroyed
29	**A** maintain	**B** support	**C** hold	**D** encourage
30	**A** fixing	**B** setting	**C** putting	**D** bringing
31	**A** performance	**B** achievement	**C** completion	**D** production
32	**A** hurried	**B** advanced	**C** forwarded	**D** accelerated
33	**A** exact	**B** correct	**C** accurate	**D** definite

PART FIVE

Questions 34–45

- Read the text below about a company's approach to social responsibility.
- In most of the lines (**34–45**), there is one extra word. It is either grammatically incorrect or does not fit in with the meaning of the text. Some lines, however, are correct.
- If a line is correct, write **CORRECT** on your Answer Sheet.
- If there is an extra word in the line, write **the extra word** in CAPITAL LETTERS on your Answer Sheet.
- The exercise begins with two examples (**0** and **00**).

Examples:	**0**	C	O	R	R	E	C	T		
	00	A	S							

Elco and social responsibility

0 Elco is a leading electrical retailer based in France. The company has been involved in

00 issues of social responsibility for many years and has always aimed to achieve as a

34 positive social impact while tackling the environmental issues are raised by electrical

35 retailing. As a consequence, Elco has been an integrated approach to social and environmental

36 issues and is particularly involved it in community schemes and recycling projects. As

37 part of this commitment, Elco helps to run like a two-year programme that trains

38 people with learning difficulties to make repair domestic electrical appliances. These

39 appliances are collected by Elco from customers' homes so when new products are

40 delivered. About 10% of them are suitable for repair, leaving the other 90% to be dismantled

41 and sold them for appropriate industrial treatment. The repaired appliances are then sold on

42 the second-hand market at a low price and with a one-year guarantee. Elco is also

43 currently working to reduce in the impact its own transport system has on the

44 environment. Drivers attend training sessions, which offered in partnership with car suppliers

45 and transport companies, to learn from how to drive in a way that respects the environment.

WRITING   45 minutes

PART ONE

- The multinational company you work for is arranging its annual conference for Human Resources managers.
- Write an **email** to the company's Human Resources managers:
  - informing them of the date of the conference
  - explaining why it is important for them to attend
  - saying what they must do if they would like to make a presentation.
- Write **40–50** words.

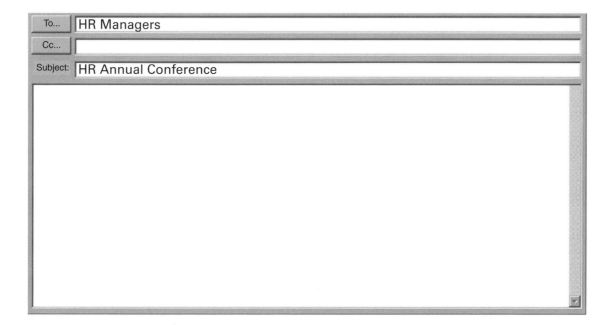

To... | HR Managers

Cc... |

Subject: | HR Annual Conference

PART TWO

- The international retail company you work for is concerned about the performance of its New York store. Your line manager has asked you to write a proposal making recommendations for the store's future.
- Look at the information below, on which you have already made some handwritten notes.
- Then, using **all** your handwritten notes, write your **proposal**.
- Write **120–140** words.

The New York store is in a very good location, but if its performance doesn't improve, we may have to close it.

Please make some recommendations to improve these aspects of performance:

- high cost of running store
- unhappy staff
- falling sales
- poor store image

should keep open

suggest how to reduce

recommend something

make suggestion

new store design needed

LISTENING 40 minutes (including 10 minutes' transfer time)

PART ONE

Questions 1–12

- You will hear three telephone conversations or messages.
- Write **one or two words or a number** in the numbered spaces on the notes or forms below.
- After you have listened once, replay each recording.

Conversation One

(Questions 1–4)

- Look at the note below.
- You will hear a man leaving a message about deliveries for one of his company's suppliers.

Telephone Message

Date: 10 December   **Name of caller:** Gupta Ramesh

Company: Morgan and Turnbull

Re: New delivery arrangements

Drivers to use the (1) .... gate (Station Road).

(2) .... will arrive by courier tomorrow

(place inside windscreen).

There will be no more (3) .... access to

the yard.

Drivers to go first to the (4) .... prior to

checking in.

Conversation Two

(Questions 5–8)

- Look at the form below.
- You will hear a woman phoning an architect to discuss a problem with a building project.

Bauer and Schmidt Architecture

Client Request

Client: *Speedlink – Antonia Radford*

Project: *Factory extension*

Problem:

- *installation of the* (5) .... *is running late*

- *delay at the supplier's due to a problem with* (6) .... *at the factory*

- *Speedlink can't use the* (7) .... *till everything is complete*

Action:

- *contract allows claim for* (8) .... *so tell builders Speedlink will now demand that*

Conversation Three

(Questions 9–12)

- Look at the notes below.
- You will hear a woman giving feedback to a colleague on his presentation at a conference.

Kim's feedback on my conference presentation

- Try to shorten the (9) ....

- Choose a bigger (10) .... for use in a large hall.

- Avoid getting in front of the (11) ....

- Cut down the amount of (12) ....
  during the presentation.

PART TWO

Questions 13–22

Section One

(Questions 13–17)

- You will hear five short recordings. Five people are explaining why they rejected a candidate for a job.
- For each recording, decide why the speaker rejected the candidate.
- Write one letter (**A–H**) next to the number of the recording.
- Do not use any letter more than once.
- After you have listened once, replay the recording.

13 ....

14 ....

15 ....

16 ....

17 ....

A	lack of relevant experience
B	poor leadership skills
C	lack of motivation
D	lack of long-term commitment
E	too independent
F	lack of formal qualifications
G	poor communication skills
H	poor references

Section Two

(Questions 18–22)

- You will hear another five recordings. Five people are giving their opinion about the annual performance review process in their companies.
- For each recording, decide what the speaker thought about the performance review process.
- Write one letter (**A–H**) next to the number of the recording.
- Do not use any letter more than once.
- After you have listened once, replay the recording.

18 ....

19 ....

20 ....

21 ....

22 ....

A	It was useful for increasing output.
B	It helped me to make a difficult decision.
C	I used it to improve my career prospects.
D	It increased my confidence.
E	It was an opportunity to speak my mind.
F	It was effective because it was short.
G	I used it to collect valuable data for future use.
H	It was a chance to exchange ideas.

PART THREE

Questions 23–30

● You will hear Desmond Butler, owner of Klikset, talking about how he created a successful toy company.
● For each question (**23–30**), mark one letter (**A**, **B** or **C**) for the correct answer.
● After you have listened once, replay the recording.

23 Desmond Butler was dissatisfied working with his father's company because

    A   the market share was declining.
    B   his earning potential was limited.
    C   there was little room for expansion.

24 Desmond Butler came up with the idea of Klikset while he was

    A   producing some plastic connectors.
    B   researching different plastic toys.
    C   playing with plastic straws.

25 His original intention was to use another company to

    A   manufacture the toy.
    B   market the toy.
    C   develop the toy.

26 Whilst producing the prototype, Desmond was

    A   confident of instant success.
    B   worried about failing.
    C   determined to continue.

27 Before establishing the Klikset company, Desmond

    A   became a buyer for a big toy company.
    B   worked in a toy factory.
    C   accepted a job working in a toy shop.

28 Before hearing Desmond's presentation, Jim Taylor, a customer, thought that

    A   the product would fail to sell.
    B   the business plan needed developing.
    C   the idea had potential.

29   Desmond joined forces with Elto because he wanted

    A   to use their design department.
    B   to export his product.
    C   to sell half his company.

30   Desmond believes the way to succeed is by

    A   being prepared to take risks.
    B   making quick decisions.
    C   producing very detailed plans.

You now have 10 minutes to transfer your answers to your Answer Sheet.

SPEAKING   14 minutes

SAMPLE SPEAKING TASKS

PART ONE

In this part, the interlocutor asks questions to each of the candidates in turn.
You have to give information about yourself and express personal opinions.

PART TWO

In this part of the test, you are asked to give a short talk on a business topic. You
have to choose one of the topics from the three below and then talk for about one
minute. You have one minute to prepare your ideas.

> **A: What is important when . . . ?**
>
> Deciding whether to visit a trade fair
> - Type of products displayed
> - Number of exhibitors
> -
> -

> **B: What is important when . . . ?**
>
> Selecting an advertising agency
> - Agency fees
> - Agency staff
> -
> -

> **C: What is important when . . . ?**
>
> Producing a marketing plan
> - Identifying target customers
> - Setting a budget
> -
> -

PART THREE

In this part of the test, you are given a discussion topic. You have 30 seconds to look at the task prompt, an example of which is below, and then about three minutes to discuss the topic with your partner. After that, the examiner will ask you more questions related to the topic.

For **two** candidates

Late Payments

The manufacturing company you work for is experiencing cash flow problems due to delays in receiving payments from customers.

You have been asked to suggest ways of dealing with the situation.

Discuss the situation together and decide:

- what would be the best way of approaching the customers who owe you money

- how the company could discourage customers from paying late in future.

For **three** candidates

Late Payments

The manufacturing company you work for is experiencing cash flow problems due to delays in receiving payments from customers.

You have been asked to suggest ways of dealing with the situation.

Discuss the situation together and decide:

- what would be the best way of approaching the customers who owe you money

- how the company could discourage customers from paying late in future

- how the company could make it easier for customers to make payments.

Follow-on questions

- Why do you think companies sometimes delay payments?

- Do you think business customers pay bills more quickly than private customers? (Why?/Why not?)

- Do you think cash flow problems are more damaging for small companies or for large companies? (Why?)

- How important are good relations between suppliers and their customers? (Why?)

- Do you think it's better for a company to have a few large customers or lots of smaller ones? (Why?)

KEY

Test 1   Reading

Part 1

1 C   2 D   3 A   4 B   5 C   6 D   7 A

Part 2

8 E   9 C   10 F   11 D   12 B

Part 3

13 C   14 A   15 D   16 A   17 B   18 C

Part 4

19 A   20 A   21 D   22 C   23 D   24 C   25 C   26 A
27 A   28 D   29 B   30 B   31 C   32 D   33 C

Part 5

34 IS   35 CORRECT 36 ANY 37 AS   38 CORRECT 39 UP
40 ONLY   41 AND   42 A   43 CORRECT 44 WHICH   45 TO

Test 1   Writing

Part 1

Sample A

> The money that spend on our company's courier services rising rapidly these days. A detailed plan should be made by each department on spending on courier services. Certain people should be pointed to check the money spending. All the saved money would be used to buy new office equipment.

Scales	Mark	Commentary
Content	4	Content is relevant to the task and the target reader would be informed but content element 2 is not entirely clear.
Communicative Achievement	3	The email is written in an appropriate register, holds the reader's attention and generally communicates straightforward ideas (*A detailed plan should be made.*).
Organisation	3	The text is coherent, with content addressed in a logical order.
Language	3	Uses some complex grammatical forms with control (*money would be used to buy new office equipment*) but other sentences are less successful (*Certain people should be pointed to check*) and (*The money that spend on our company's courier services …*). Errors do not impede communication.

Sample B

> As I know that spending on courier services has risen recently, as all the staff regarded the time when given for a useless things, and some people in our company enjoyed the services endless, for instance buying everything useless on holidays. To save money, we have to take some measure in controll much which is spend on courier services. Every one who wants to enjoy services must come to the manager and accountant for permission.

Scales	Mark	Commentary
Content	1	A number of irrelevances are present (*regarded the time when given for a useless things*), and content element 3 is not adequately addressed. The target reader would be minimally informed.
Communicative Achievement	1	Uses email conventions to communicate ideas in a generally appropriate way, although lacks concision.
Organisation	2	The email is connected despite a very long first sentence and uses some cohesive devices (*as*; *and*; *for instance*).
Language	1	Uses everyday vocabulary and simple grammatical forms (*we have to*; *Every one who wants to … must …*). Errors are noticeable and at times impede communication (*buying everything useless on holidays*) although generally meaning can still be determined.

Part 2

Sample C

> The purpose of this report is to show the results of our recent customer survey.
>
> Firstly 70% of our customer found our staff unfriendly. This should be no longer the case, because new training for the staff will start next month.
>
> Concerning our product range, we have to improve our diversification, because 38% of our customer found it poor. We should add some new products like Hi-Fi and electronics.
>
> Regarding the opening hours, customer found it very good. The reason is that we are now open till 9pm every day.
>
> Concerning the parking we are progressing quite rapidly with the construction of the new parking area, so this would be no longer a problem, and in the same time the new store layout should be ready next month.
>
> In conclusion, we are on track with all our project.

Scales	Mark	Commentary
Content	5	All content is relevant and the points are expanded where appropriate so that the target reader is fully informed.
Communicative Achievement	5	Uses the conventions of a report effectively to hold the target reader's attention (*The purpose of this report*; *In conclusion*). The report communicates straightforward and complex ideas clearly and the register is appropriately formal.
Organisation	4	Uses a variety of features which organise the ideas well (*because*; *Concerning*; *Regarding*; *The reason is*; <u>*this*</u> *would*).
Language	4	A range of less common vocabulary and some complex structures is used (*This should be no longer the case*; *we have to improve our diversification*; *we are on track*). Errors are present (*70% of our customer*; *rapidely*; *in the same time*) but these do not impede communication.

Sample D

Dear Sir

The aim of this report is to analyze the customer satisfaction to our store and how to improve our services.

According to the survey, 70% of the customers thought bad of our staff friendliness. I think new training for staff should be carried out and help us to improve customers satisfaction. We should increase our category of goods to attract customers due to about 40% of them thought that there was not large range of goods for them. Due to the prelong opening hours on business, nearly 90% of them was satisfied with this aspect.

In addition, some customers felt it difficult finding thinks. I suggest new store layout should be completed by the end of next month. And our new parking place will come to use in one week, the parking problems would be solved soon.

That's my analyzis on the survey, if you have any problems, please call me.

Yours sincerely

Scales	Mark	Commentary
Content	2	Content element 1 is not entirely clear (*new training for staff should be carried out*). Content element 2 lacks expansion on what type of product (*we should increase our category of goods*) and *prelong hours* in content element 3 is unclear. The target reader would be partially informed.
Communicative Achievement	3	Report writing conventions are generally used appropriately (*The aim of this report*; *According to the survey*). Register is sometimes inconsistent (*That's my analyzis*).
Organisation	3	Generally well-organised with some suitable linking (*In addition*) and use of pronouns to avoid repetition (*we / us* for the company and *them* for the customers).
Language	2	Uses a range of simple and complex forms. Errors are noticeable (*thought bad of our staff*; *there was not large range of goods*; *prelong*) but meaning can still be determined.

Test 1 Listening

Part 1

1 (RETAIL) EXHIBITION
2 STANDS
3 PRICE(-)LISTS
4 (PRESS) CONFERENCE
5 MIDDLEMISS / MIDDLE MISS
6 SALES EXEC(UTIVE)
7 (COMPANY) PRESENTATION
8 REFEREES
9 (THE) SHAREHOLDERS
10 (THE) (PLANNED) MERGER
11 THE (COMBINED) SALES
12 EXPECTED SAVINGS

Part 2

13 E   14 B   15 H   16 F   17 C   18 D   19 H   20 C   21 A   22 F

Part 3

23 B   24 C   25 C   26 B   27 B   28 C   29 A   30 C

Tapescript

Listening Test 1

This is the Business English Certificate Vantage 5, Listening Test 1.

Part One. Questions 1 to 12.

You will hear three telephone conversations or messages.

Write one or two words or a number in the numbered spaces on the notes or forms below.

After you have listened once, replay each recording.

Conversation One. Questions 1 to 4.

Look at the note below.

You will hear a man calling his office.

You have 15 seconds to read through the note.

[pause]

Now listen, and fill in the spaces.

Man: Thank you for calling Andersons International. Our offices are closed at the moment. Please leave your name, number and message after the tone.

Man: Hello, Martin Hayes here – I've just arrived. The journey was fine, no problems at the airport. I've arrived at the Retail Exhibition – the building's really impressive! The only problem is, the stands that we sent by air cargo last week are missing – the computer's arrived, and the posters are here, though. Can you get onto the transport people first thing in the morning to track them down and get them here by tomorrow evening at the very latest? Stress how urgent it is! Also, I've just unpacked the brochures and realised we haven't got enough price-lists to give out with them. We'll need another five hundred; use a courier to get them out here – the day after tomorrow at the latest. Call me back when you know what's happening. I'm at the press conference all morning today, but you can get me during lunch. I'll speak to you again later.

[pause]

Now listen to the recording again.

[pause]

Conversation Two. Questions 5 to 8.

Look at the note below.

You will hear a woman calling about a job application.

You have 15 seconds to read through the note.

[pause]

Now listen, and fill in the spaces.

Woman: Oh, hello, can I speak to Jill Croft, please?
Man: I'm sorry, but she's not here at the moment. Can I take a message?
Woman: Oh, please. It's Sarah Middlemiss here. M-I-double D-L-E-M-I-double S . . . from Pegasus Communications Ltd.
Man: Thanks. What's the message?
Woman: Well, I'm the personnel manager here at Pegasus . . . it's regarding the position of sales executive Jill has applied for. It's just to let her know that before we arrange interview dates, we're inviting applicants to a company presentation on the twenty-eighth. We'll confirm this, of course, by letter.
Man: Fine – I'll let her know that.
Woman: One other thing – we've received her application and curriculum vitae, but can't find any mention of her referees. Could you ask her to let us have their details as soon as possible?
Man: OK – I've noted that down.
Woman: Thanks very much for your help.
Man: No problem. Bye for now . . .

[pause]

Now listen to the recording again.

[pause]

Conversation Three. Questions 9 to 12.

Look at the note below.

You will hear a man phoning about some arrangements for a meeting.

You have 15 seconds to read through the note.

[pause]

Now listen, and fill in the spaces.

[pause]

Woman: Hello. Sales. Can I help you?
Man: Oh, hello. Is Lauren O'Neil there?
Woman: I'm sorry, but she's at lunch right now. Can I take a message?
Man: Um . . . OK. It's Chris Darcy here, from Human Resources. I'm phoning about next week's . . .

Woman:	. . . Hang on, I just need to get a pen. Right, here we are. So, it's Chris Darcy from HR, and it's about . . .
Man:	The shareholders' meeting next week.
Woman:	OK. And what shall I tell Lauren?
Man:	Tell Lauren the board's decided to make an official statement about the planned merger. I know we weren't going to, but they've changed their mind.
Woman:	Oh . . . Yes, that's interesting.
Man:	Mm, but not entirely unexpected. Anyway, the MD needs Lauren to put together a presentation showing the combined sales of the newly-merged group.
Woman:	OK. I've got that. Is there anything else?
Man:	Yes, tell her that I'll handle the presentation about HR issues, but could Lauren also include something about expected savings in her part of the presentation?
Woman:	OK. I'll give her the message.
Man:	That's great. Thanks very much.

[pause]

Now listen to the recording again.

[pause]

That is the end of Part One. You now have 20 seconds to check your answers.

[pause]

Part Two. Questions 13 to 22.

Section One. Questions 13 to 17.

You will hear five short recordings.

For each recording, decide which aspect of working conditions the speaker is talking about.

Write one letter (A–H) next to the number of the recording.

Do not use any letter more than once.

After you have listened once, replay the recordings.

You have 15 seconds to read the list A–H.

[pause]

Now listen, and decide which aspect of working conditions each speaker is talking about.

[pause]

Thirteen
The hours vary – sometimes lunchtimes, sometimes late afternoons. We all feel we've improved our skills or picked up new ones which will benefit us in the future in some way. Outside providers are contracted to come in and they've been very good, very professional. There's been a range of things on offer, too. We're given vouchers which we use in a way to pay for the sessions, choosing what to do and how many hours to put in.

[pause]

Fourteen
Things have improved a lot since I started working here. We're all more aware now of potential risks and of the correct procedures for everything. For example, reporting anything that isn't working properly, having the appropriate clothing, things like that. We know what to do now, and who to go to. There are regular checks on equipment, too, so that problems are less likely to happen in the first place.

Key

[pause]

Fifteen
Well, despite talks with senior management, we've been unable so far to agree on something which all my staff can accept. Management know we have a fair case and that we've waited a long time compared to other departments, who were awarded rises last year. So it's not as if they're against the idea itself . . . as I say, we've just got to get a final figure which staff will be happy with.

[pause]

Sixteen
There are various stages we go through. We try first to reassure staff and give them the opportunity to present their side. We like first to deal with things within the organisation – staff know action won't be taken until the case has been thoroughly investigated. Of course, problems can arise from lots of things – anything from poor timekeeping or inappropriate dress to actual breach of contract. Dismissal would be the very last course of action and all employees have the right to appeal even then.

[pause]

Seventeen
I very much like the system we have – I like the opportunities it gives me for other things. Everyone's at work for the agreed essential time, but we all have some choice each side of this. I keep my own record, and it means I can fit in other things, like medical appointments. I like to feel I've got some control over my professional life and I need to be able to plan. It may not suit everyone, but it certainly works for me.

[pause]

Now listen to the recordings again.

[pause]

Section Two. Questions 18 to 22.

You will hear another five recordings.

For each recording, decide what each speaker is trying to do.

Write one letter (A–H) next to the number of the recording.

Do not use any letter more than once.

After you have listened once, replay the recordings.

You have 15 seconds to read the list A–H.

[pause]

Now listen, and decide what each speaker is trying to do.

[pause]

Eighteen
I take your point Brian. I know that since George left you've had to take on some of his tasks which were not in your original job description. However, you were allocated seventy-five per cent of Suzie's time to deal with the paperwork, so I feel that the situation, although not ideal, is manageable and in this financial climate any further expenditure, any rise, however well deserved, might damage the company's future and, I am sure you'll agree, that's too risky.

[pause]

Nineteen
I wanted to have a word about the departmental budget forecast you asked me to draw up. I totally agree with you on the need for working out the future expenditure well in advance, it's only that since

we've never done this forecast in such a detailed way before, it's taking us much longer than I expected. Would it be acceptable to the board if I deferred the submission date by a fortnight?

[pause]

Twenty
May I come in here? Thank you. I think Tom's last point was very valuable. We mustn't forget how important it is to make a really good impression when we launch the new T-six engine at the Air Show in Paris. Although we're very familiar with the engine's specifications and performance data, we aren't skilled at giving polished multi-media presentations which the audience expects nowadays. Tom's right. I think we should consider hiring in a professional from a marketing company.

[pause]

Twenty-one
I know why you want Smithson's – they're the biggest in the field and they've got years of experience. The disadvantage is the price. They're the best so they can charge what they like. Personally, I'd prefer to go for someone local like Mackays. They're small, so we could negotiate a favourable deal, and I'm sure they'd do their best to deliver the stuff on time and help us if we had an emergency job and needed extra materials.

[pause]

Twenty-two
Jones and Sons have always been our haulage company and they've been reliable. But things changed when Michael Jones took over. The service wasn't so efficient and then last month two trucks were four days late on a delivery with no explanation and no apologies. As a result, we lost a new customer. I refuse to just accept that financial loss. So write to Jones please, demanding ten per cent of our expected profit from that contract. I think it's only fair.

[pause]

Now listen to the recordings again.

[pause]

That is the end of Part Two.

[pause]

Part Three. Questions 23 to 30.

You will hear a radio interview with a leading industrialist and business consultant, Philip Spencer.

For each question, 23–30, mark one letter (A, B or C) for the correct answer.

After you have listened once, replay the recording.

You have 45 seconds to read through the questions.

[pause]

Now listen, and mark A, B or C.

[pause]

Woman:	. . . And now let's meet Philip Spencer, one of Britain's top industrialists, and hear about his experiences and ideas on improving company performance . . . welcome, Philip.
Man:	Thanks, Gemma. Good to be here.
Woman:	Philip, you're famous for your unique approach when called in to advise companies . . .
Man:	Well, I'm certainly very generous with my advice! I always acknowledge genuine effort wherever possible – it is important to do so; but my job isn't to manage the company, it's to hunt down underlying weaknesses in the systems; that's what I'm trained to do.

Woman:	Your visit to Manson's received a very mixed response, didn't it?
Man:	Well, yes. Following my first visit, they'd researched the market more deeply and had improved product quality considerably, but, on my return, I blamed their failures on the ancient assembly line which they'd still done nothing about, despite my report, and which by now had led to a ten-year waiting list for their customers. The company was so upset by the comments I made during my second visit that they didn't invite me back!
Woman:	Another of your consultations took you to Criterion Glass, a family-run business ...
Man:	Yes. Their troubles started with an over-concentration on the actual making of the product, on the craftsmanship involved, without asking themselves whether there was still enough of a market for that type of product. Prices needed to be more competitive too, something they hadn't considered sufficiently.
Woman:	As you said, you're famous for your advice to industry, but for a long time you were not at all successful in business yourself, were you?
Man:	True! The first two organisations I headed went into liquidation! They were both relatively new companies, though, without a long history and were trying to establish their brand name. People had tried to warn me, of course. The resources were there – that wasn't the problem – but I just couldn't get things to work – basically because financial services just isn't my field.
Woman:	You enjoy a strong public image, with your unusual choice of clothes, etcetera. Why did you start to cultivate this original style?
Man:	Well, many people think I've developed this style just to get myself noticed, but it's really because I think my ability is what matters in business – more than my image. I like to do my own thing, so why shouldn't I please myself how I look? I know many other business people prefer to follow convention and dress more seriously – that's up to them.
Woman:	Did this help you to get one of the top jobs in the country – the chairmanship of LBI?
Man:	That's not really for me to say ... the company was in serious trouble when I joined. I think they recognised the risk-taker in me and they needed someone who wasn't afraid of change. The management had preferred to play safe until then – and this, together with their rather poor reputation, was the cause of their problems.
Woman:	Your record in the second half of your career speaks for itself, of course. Now, when you look at managers today, how effective do you think they are?
Man:	Well – there's great emphasis now on making money, which I know is what business is about, but too many managers today are interested in making money for themselves. There are a lot of strong personalities around, too, in leadership positions. But people forget that the sort of success which lasts requires close attention to every single aspect of the company, however unimportant it may appear.
Woman:	Well, you're full of energy yourself, and working harder than ever at the age of seventy ... as you reflect on your long career, have you any advice for those just starting?
Man:	Well, I've taken risks and made errors, but I've learnt it's best never to worry about things you can't do anything about. If you did your best with the information you had at the time, then you must live with your mistakes and move on.
Woman:	Philip Spencer, thank you very much indeed. Now I'll ...

[pause]

Now listen to the recording again.

[pause]

That is the end of Part Three. You now have ten minutes to transfer your answers to your Answer Sheet.

[pause]

Note: Teacher, stop the recording here and time ten minutes. Remind students when there is **one** minute remaining.

That is the end of the test.

Test 2   Reading

Part 1

1 D   2 B   3 D   4 C   5 B   6 A   7 C

Part 2

8 B   9 E   10 A   11 D   12 C

Part 3

13 C   14 B   15 D   16 A   17 A   18 C

Part 4

19 C	20 A	21 B	22 C	23 A	24 D	25 D	26 B
27 D	28 B	29 C	30 A	31 D	32 A	33 D	

Part 5

34 ITSELF	35 CORRECT	36 TO	37 NO
38 WHICH	39 ABOUT	40 CORRECT	41 OF
42 WHOSE	43 RESULTING	44 CORRECT	45 SUCCEED

Test 2   Writing

Part 1

Sample A

> The marketing meeting that was scheduled for next Friday will take place on Monday. We had to change the date due to technical problems, with the computer equipment.
>
> Please note that there will be an extra presentation at the end of the meeting concerning teamwork.

Scales	Mark	Commentary
Content	5	All content is relevant to the task and the target reader would be fully informed.
Communicative Achievement	5	The email effectively communicates the message and has a natural tone which would have a positive effect on the target reader, holding their attention throughout.
Organisation	4	The text is well-organised and coherent using a number of linking devices (*that was scheduled*; *due to*).
Language	5	Uses a range of vocabulary and more complex grammatical forms with control (*will take place*; *had to change the date due to*; *Please note that there will be …*).

Sample B

> Dear colleagues
>
> Our meeting which should be held next Friday is going to be moved to Monday the following week, because the two members cannot leave work on that particular date at all.
>
> I want to inform you as well that we have another point added to the agenda, it will be the planning of our trip to the marketing seminar.

Scales	Mark	Commentary
Content	5	All the content is addressed, although content element 2 is less effective (*the two members cannot leave work on that particular date at all*) but the target reader would still be fully informed.
Communicative Achievement	4	Uses the conventions of an email to hold the target reader's attention successfully. The register is appropriate to the task, although it lacks a natural tone.
Organisation	4	The email is well-organised with a variety of organisational features including appropriate paragraphing, linking (*because*; *as well*) and use of pronouns to avoid repetition (*it will be …*).
Language	4	Uses a range of vocabulary (*particular date*; *marketing seminar*) and some complex grammatical forms are used with control (*should be held*; *to inform you as well that …*).

Part 2

Sample C

> Mr Rodich:
>
> I'm very glad to receive the information of Venture Enterprises. It is our honor if we can cooperate with your company. Our company named TG which focus on developing digital product we have also high reputation in this field with 50 years experience.
>
> We have developed a new MP3 player recently, the target consumer of this product is student. It can not only playing music but also searching on internet, which will attract many younger people. The design of this MP3 player is very fashional and friendly-user. According to our market survey, 80% of the student in college would like to try this new product. Now, we are going to launch the new product in market, which will need 2 million euros in advertisement.
>
> Our company must be a better choice for you. Our profits have increased 10% last year to 32 million euros. We will try our best to do better this year.
>
> It is grateful if you choose our company to invest. I am looking forward to hear from you.

Scales	Mark	Commentary
Content	5	All content is relevant with the points expanded appropriately (*focus on developing digital product; in this field with 50 years experience*). The target reader would be fully informed.
Communicative Achievement	3	Follows letter conventions to hold the target reader's attention and communicate the ideas. However, register and tone are not entirely appropriate (*It is our honor*; *It is grateful if you choose …*).
Organisation	4	Well-organised, using a number of organisational features including pronominal referencing (*it* for *MP3 player*; *we* for *company*).
Language	3	Uses a range of everyday business vocabulary appropriately (*target consumer*; *launch the new product*) and some complex grammatical forms (*We have developed*; *which will attract …*). However, errors are noticeable (*Our company named TG*; *is very fashional*; *friendly-user*; *80% of the student*) although they do not impede communication.

Sample D

> Dear Rodich
>
> Thanks for your letter date 28 May 2008, in which contained some information about finance. Our company is a IT company, it is a leader in the industry. It ownes 1,000 staff, and in the last year, it make 2,000 million margin.
>
> We have a good new product. It is smaller than the original product, And it will be convenicelly to peoples life.
>
> After our research, the market is very perspective. We are confidence in the market. Because of hi-tech skill, we need an investment about 4 million. We are greateful if you would like to invest to the product. I believe it is a ideal choie to choose our product to invest. Please consider the things above I mentioned.
>
> I am looking forward to hearing from you.
>
> Yours sincerely

Scales	Mark	Commentary
Content	2	Several content elements are not fully addressed. The target reader is partially informed.
Communicative Achievement	2	The letter communicates simple ideas in a generally appropriate way to hold the reader's attention (*Our company is*; *We have a good new product*).
Organisation	3	The text is generally coherent, well paragraphed, and uses a variety of cohesive devices, e.g. pronominal referencing (*Our company is a IT company, it …*; *We have a good new product. It is …*; *the things above*).
Language	1	Uses everyday vocabulary and simple grammatical forms with a degree of control (*Thank you for your letter*; *in the last year*). Errors are noticeable, but the meaning can still be determined (*We are confidence in the market*; *We are greateful if …*).

Test 2   Listening

Part 1

1 (A) FACTORY VISIT
2 ADVERTISING
3 EXPENSE CLAIMS
4 MARKETING DIRECTOR
5 (ADVERTISING / AD) CAMPAIGN
6 QUALITY CONTROL
7 (THE) (EUROPEAN) LAUNCH
8 (THE) TASK FORCE
9 AGENTS ABROAD
10 SUPPLIERS
11 NEW LOGO
12 ENTERPRISE BOARD

Part 2

13 G   14 E   15 B   16 H   17 F   18 D   19 G   20 A   21 F   22 C

Part 3

23 B   24 C   25 C   26 B   27 C   28 C   29 A   30 B

Tapescript

Listening Test 2

This is the Business English Certificate Vantage 5, Listening Test 2.

Part One. Questions 1 to 12.

You will hear three telephone conversations or messages.

Write one or two words or a number in the numbered spaces on the notes or forms below.

After you have listened once, replay each recording.

Conversation One. Questions 1 to 4.

Look at the notes below.

You will hear a woman giving information about a timetable.

You have 15 seconds to read through the notes.

[pause]

Now listen, and fill in the spaces.

[pause]

Man:	Hello, Geoff Wilson.
Woman:	Oh, hello. It's Myra from Barlings, Personnel Department. I've got some information about the arrangements for you and the other new salesmen next week.
Man:	Oh right.
Woman:	Well now, on Monday, rather than sending you out on a tour of client companies right away, we've decided on a factory visit. OK?
Man:	Sounds a good idea.
Woman:	Tuesday, there will be some training in the product development lab. Then on Wednesday, you'll need to know how other departments work as well as sales. Advertising is always busy in the afternoon, so they will be better able to answer questions in the morning.
Man:	Right. What about sorting out the admin?
Woman:	Well the most important thing is expense claims. So after lunch that day, someone in accounts will go over them with you. The rest will be covered during training.
Man:	What about the marketing director – will I see him?
Woman:	Oh yes. He has a weekly briefing on Thursday mornings – we've put you down to attend that. In fact, the Managing Director sometimes comes so you may even meet him there or we'll fix something up for the following week.
Man:	OK. See you next week. Goodbye.
Woman:	Goodbye.

[pause]

Now listen to the recording again.

[pause]

Key

Conversation Two. Questions 5 to 8.

Look at the note below.

You will hear a woman leaving a message about some problems with her company's new product.

You have 15 seconds to read through the note.

[pause]

Now listen, and fill in the spaces.

Man:	Marketing. Joe speaking.
Woman:	Hi Joe. Is Jamie there?
Man:	No, sorry. He's got a day off today. Can I help?
Woman:	I need to leave him an urgent message. This is Alice from Product Development.
Man:	OK Alice. Go ahead.
Woman:	It's about the advertising campaign Jamie's working on for the new Trimco HP-four.
Man:	Right, got that. Is something wrong? You sound worried.
Woman:	I am. The quality control people have turned up some serious defects across a significant number of units.
Man:	Oh no. So what's being done about it?
Woman:	The production department have got their best people working on it, but it means we won't be able to meet the target for the European launch that was supposed to be next month.
Man:	Next month! That's close.
Woman:	It certainly is. There's an emerging plan to try to save the programme, and they've set up a task force based in Berlin. I'm part of it, so I've got to go out there.
Man:	Right. I'll tell Jamie.
Woman:	Good. I'll be in touch as soon as I can, but he must try to hold everything for now.
Man:	OK. Good luck.
Woman:	Thanks. I'll need it.

[pause]

Now listen to the recording again.

[pause]

Conversation Three. Questions 9 to 12.

Look at the notes below.

You will hear a manager telling a colleague about what happened in a meeting.

You have 15 seconds to read through the notes.

[pause]

Now listen, and fill in the spaces.

Woman:	Leon, it's Emily. About the web development, we had a meeting while you were away . . .
Man:	Yuh.
Woman:	Actually, it was interesting to find out the current situation. The website is still underused. It's getting some hits from customers, though not as many as from agents abroad.
Man:	Oh?
Woman:	Don't worry. Customers will come on board as the net grows. But what we have to concentrate on is making the site more appealing to suppliers, so they have a better picture of what we are about.
Man:	More inclusive . . .

Woman:	There's a working party looking into that. Meanwhile, there's a couple of small changes. Since the brochures are going out with the new logo on them, we thought that it should be posted on the site too.
Man:	Makes sense . . .
Woman:	And the present set of links, group companies and international businesses news bulletin, will also include the Enterprise Board. It's a two-way process, so we should get hits from there too.
Man:	Yes . . . I'd also wondered about . . .

[pause]

Now listen to the recording again.

[pause]

That is the end of Part One. You now have 20 seconds to check your answers.

[pause]

Part Two. Questions 13 to 22.

Section One. Questions 13 to 17.

You will hear five short recordings about delivery problems.

For each recording, decide which problem the speaker talks about.

Write one letter (A–H) next to the number of the recording.

Do not use any letter more than once.

After you have listened once, replay the recordings.

You have 15 seconds to read the list A–H.

[pause]

Now listen, and decide which problem each speaker talks about.

[pause]

Thirteen
Once I needed to replace our office chairs, so I compared products in several manufacturers' brochures, chose the model that best suited our purposes, and ordered ten of them. Well, they were supposed to be delivered within twenty-eight days, and when they finally arrived, practically at the last minute in fact, we found that the description in the brochure had given quite a false impression of them. We sent them back, and had a lot of trouble with the manufacturer.

[pause]

Fourteen
I run a small beauty salon, just the one site, so my orders are quite small quantities compared with the big chains. But I still expect my suppliers to provide a high level of customer service. And with all the packaging that's available these days, it should be easy enough to ensure consignments are properly protected, but more than once I've had to return goods because when they arrived they weren't in a fit state to be used.

[pause]

Fifteen
We're a small printing firm, so of course we get regular supplies of ink and paper. The way it works, we sign a contract with a supplier for a year at a time, and they send the same quantity each month,

unless we phone to change it, of course. Well, one year we didn't renew the contract with our regular ink supplier, but the month after it expired, they sent the usual order. We weren't impressed. I must say.

[pause]

Sixteen

I'm responsible for centralised ordering for a multi-site organisation – we're a chain of builders' merchants – and it's amazing how often suppliers get confused. Of course we double check the paperwork before sending it to them, but even so, things happen like the time bathroom equipment arrived at head office instead of one of the branches, which was desperate for the goods. And once, boxes of mouse mats meant for head office turned up along with window frames and bricks.

[pause]

Seventeen

I'm a store manager in a chain that sells arts and crafts equipment. Our central warehouse orders goods boxed up in small amounts ready to go straight onto the shelves of the stores. For example, poster paints usually come in boxes of ten. Everything's then distributed to the branches when it's required. But in the last delivery, the warehouse received the right number of pens, but in boxes of a thousand! It took ages to sort it out.

[pause]

Now listen to the recordings again.

[pause]

Section Two. Questions 18 to 22.

You will hear another five recordings. Five people are talking about project management.

For each recording, decide what action the speaker is recommending.

Write one letter (A–H) next to the number of the recording.

Do not use any letter more than once.

After you have listened once, replay the recordings.

You have 15 seconds to read the list A–H.

[pause]

Now listen, and decide what action each speaker is recommending.

[pause]

Eighteen

I can tell you from my own experience that the most important thing in project management is not to try to do everything yourself. That'll lead to problems sooner rather than later. You must plan which tasks you really need to do yourself and then delegate responsibility for each of the other tasks to others. You should of course, make sure the members of your team have the initiative and flexibility necessary for such responsibilities.

[pause]

Nineteen

I think, it's absolutely crucial that all the people to whom you've delegated responsibilities should get together at least once a month so that you can all share information about how your own bits of the project are going. If you don't do that, then it's easy to assume something has been done by someone else when it hasn't – after all, not everyone has the same level of motivation. Email contact is great, of course, but nothing beats face-to-face communication.

[pause]

Twenty
You have to get off to a good start which means you have to be absolutely clear about what your aims are right from the start. These should be discussed with the team and should be put in writing so that everyone shares full knowledge about the precise parameters of the project. I know from several projects I've been involved with that confusion about goals often leads to problems early on, problems which could very easily have been prevented.

[pause]

Twenty-one
When you're working on a new project, you have to delegate, of course. But, if anything starts to go wrong you should handle it yourself. As project manager, it is up to you to keep a close eye on how things are progressing. You should try to predict any difficulties and sort them out immediately so the project can move on. There are many tasks that can be handed over to other people, but not this.

[pause]

Twenty-two
Planning things in detail is, of course, vital. However, it makes sense to ensure that your initial plan incorporates a degree of adaptability. You and your project team can't assume that circumstances will stay the same for ever, and so it makes sense for your plan not to be so rigid that it cannot take account of any developments and changes in circumstance. It should not, of course, need to stray from its basic objectives.

[pause]

Now listen to the recordings again.

[pause]

That is the end of Part Two.

[pause]

Part Three. Questions 23 to 30.

You will hear a radio interview with Donald White, the author of a book about running board meetings.

For each question, 23–30, mark one letter (A, B or C) for the correct answer.

After you have listened once, replay the recording.

You have 45 seconds to read through the questions.

[pause]

Now listen, and mark A, B or C.

[pause]

Woman:	Good afternoon, Donald. Your book, *The Successful Board Meeting*, will, I'm sure, soon be compulsory reading for directors. Please tell us first what you see as the chief role of the board meeting. Do people attending them really play the power games we see in TV dramas?
Man:	That can happen, of course. Certainly, people who don't attend them are often cynical about board meetings. The tendency is to see them as a place where fat cats congratulate each other on their success. But that public perception is false – they're actually far more frequently used as the place where new strategic ideas are discussed.
Woman:	So what advice would you give a company wanting to make board meetings more successful? Is it just a matter of making sure the right people are on the board?
Man:	That's certainly important. As well as having someone who is skilled at chairing meetings effectively. But, I'm with a chairman I heard about the other day – he cancelled a board

meeting because the papers weren't ready. It is no good inviting people to a meeting when they haven't got time to consider the issues in advance.

Woman: Then the meeting will be more effective, won't it?

Man: That's right. It also saves time as the presenters at the meeting don't have to formally present the conclusions of their report and can instead focus on fielding any questions that arise. This means there'll be more time for the chair to lead a more productive discussion of any issues raised by the report in general.

Woman: You've mentioned the chair several times. Obviously the choice of chairperson is crucial to a board's effectiveness. Who do you think makes the best chair?

Man: The role of the chair is to support the chief executive and help him do the best job possible but not to do it for him. Often an outgoing executive takes on the role of the chair, but they can find it a difficult part to play if they are not really ready yet to give up the reins – so I'd go for someone who's heading for the top. An inexperienced business person, though, is a bit of a risk as the skills needed by a chair do have to be learnt.

Woman: What qualities and skills does the chair need then?

Man: It has to be someone who can resist the desire to impose his own will on the board. He must ensure all opinions are covered and must be able to keep people calm at stressful moments. He should be able to point out the strengths in any argument and help the board come to the best decision possible.

Woman: I suppose the agenda is another important factor in running a successful meeting?

Man: Yes, it's extraordinary how little time is devoted to prioritising what goes on the agenda. It's often drawn up by a secretary from a standard list because the people attending the meeting are supposedly spending their time focusing on more important matters. I think many senior executives think it's an administrative matter that is beneath them.

Woman: So what'd you suggest?

Man: Well, for a start, it can be more sensible to think through agendas on an annual rather than an individual meeting basis so that routine issues are on the agenda for just a couple of the year's meetings rather than for every one of them. A lot of routine points are there because they are always there and people then get bogged down discussing those with the result that there isn't enough time to discuss what really needs to be talked through at this high level.

Woman: Any other key advice you'd give?

Man: Well, yes, I'd remind people that what happens after the meeting is of great importance too. A meeting is only as good as its follow-up. Ideally, minutes should be distributed within twenty-four hours of the meeting both to people who were at the meeting and those who were not able to attend. Otherwise people who were there won't be able to check whether the minutes represent a true and accurate version of what was said. And they must be accurate so they can be signed off quickly at the next board meeting.

Woman: Thank you.

[pause]

Now listen to the recording again.

[pause]

That is the end of Part Three. You now have ten minutes to transfer your answers to your Answer Sheet.

[pause]

Note: Teacher, stop the recording here and time ten minutes. Remind students when there is **one** minute remaining.

[pause]

That is the end of the test.

Test 3 Reading

Part 1

1 B   2 A   3 C   4 D   5 B   6 D   7 A

Part 2

8 F   9 C   10 A   11 D   12 E

Part 3

13 B   14 C   15 B   16 D   17 D   18 A

Part 4

19 D	20 B	21 C	22 A	23 D	24 A	25 D	26 C
27 A	28 B	29 B	30 C	31 B	32 B	33 A	

Part 5

34 COST	35 ARE	36 UNTIL	37 CORRECT	38 MADE	39 SO
40 CORRECT	41 WHICH	42 CORRECT	43 OF	44 ONE	45 AGAIN

Test 3   Writing

Part 1

Sample A

> Dear all,
>
> As you already know we had some problems with the new computer system. The new server broke down yesterday. Please accept our sincere apologies. We now can change the server and it will be possible to work with the new system from next Tuesday on.
>
> Kind regards

Scales	Mark	Commentary
Content	5	All content is relevant to the task and the target reader would be fully informed.
Communicative Achievement	5	Communicates the message effectively. The format, register and natural tone (*As you already know*) are all appropriate to the task and would have a positive effect on the reader.
Organisation	5	The email is well-organised with the content expressed in a logical order within the two paragraphs.
Language	5	The email uses a good range of lexis (*sincere apologies*; *server broke down*) and some complex grammatical forms (*it will be possible to*).

Sample B

> I am sorry to inform you that there has been a delay setting up a new computer system.
>
> We cannot set up the new system without stable electricity facility, so the new system will be ready until next Monday after we improved the electricity facility.

Scales	Mark	Commentary
Content	5	All the content is relevant to the task and the target reader would be informed.
Communicative Achievement	3	Uses email conventions to communicate straightforward ideas (*I am sorry to inform you that ...*).
Organisation	3	The email is well-organised with the content expressed in a logical order. Some organisational features are used (*so*; *after*).
Language	4	Some complex grammatical forms are used (*has been a delay setting up*) and a range of vocabulary including less common lexis (*stable electricity facility*). However, errors are sometimes present in more complex structures (*the new system will be ready until next Monday*) but these do not impede communication.

Part 2

Sample C

> Report on sales
>
> Introduction:
> This report aims to suggest stragies to improve television (TV) sales.
>
> Findings:
> According to statistics, retail sales of all the regions have fallen over the previous 3 months. But I have confidence that the customers' needs to our products will increase in next 6 months.
>
> Conclusions:
> As a result of analysis above, I will give suggestions as follows:
> * Firstly, we can offer discounts to customers, so that they can buy more products at more reasonable prices.
> * Secondly, we can launch a new advertising campaign in golden week, inviting some medias, such as local press, national press and magazines, to progandize our products.
> * Thirdly, as more and more customers want to watch movies at home, we should improve our TV's audio effect and give them a real cinema feel.
>
> Recommendation:
> Through those stragies I mentioned above, I believe we can win this sales war.

Scales	Mark	Commentary
Content	5	All the content is relevant to the task and expanded appropriately. The target reader would be fully informed.
Communicative Achievement	4	The format and register are appropriate for a report. The text communicates straightforward ideas (*we can offer discounts to customers*) and holds the target reader's attention effectively.
Organisation	5	The report is well-organised with a clear introduction and recommendation. The writer uses a variety of organisational features including sequencing words (*Firstly*; *Secondly*), headings (*Introduction*; *Findings*; *Conclusions*) and bullet points to organise the report effectively.
Language	4	Uses a range of simple and complex grammatical structures (*sales ... have fallen ...*; *they can buy more products at more reasonable prices*) and a range of vocabulary, including less common lexis (*cinema feel*; *sales war*). Errors are present but do not impede communication (*customers' needs to our products*; *progandize*; *stragies*).

Sample D

Mr Mike:

I have recieved your letter on Monday 10 Apirl. As you pointed that we have been a fall over 3 months we hold a meeting, discussing what make it happened.

Since all retail sales fallen due to the ecnomic criss, it also infuluce our sales. But we find some suggestion for increasing sales of our products and promise we will improve this situation in next 6 months.

First, we would like to give special offers for customers such as diliver our product who buy it into their home.

Second, put some new advertising campaign and send it to customers mail box.

Then, we decied to improe technology and design to make new product in order to appeal customer.

If you have any further question, please contact us, we will reply as soon as possible.

Your Sincerly

Scales	Mark	Commentary
Content	2	The target reader is only partly informed due to minor omissions. Content element 5 is not adequately addressed (*we decied to improe technology ... to appeal customer*).
Communicative Achievement	2	The register is generally appropriate to the task. However, the genre is not entirely appropriate for a report (*Mr Mike*). Straightforward ideas are communicated.
Organisation	4	The report is well-organised using a variety of organisational features and cohesive devices (*First*; *Second*; *But*; *Since*) and *it* for *the fall in sales* and *we* for *the company*.
Language	1	Everyday business vocabulary (*retail sales*) and simple grammatical forms are used (*we will improve this situation*; *we would like to ...*). Errors are noticeable but the meaning can still generally be determined (*the ecnomic criss ... infuluce our sales*; *diliver*; *improe technology*).

Test 3   Listening

Part 1

1 CANCELLED
2 12:30 / 12-30 (PM) / HALF PAST TWELVE / TWELVE THIRTY
3 (A) LUNCH (VENUE)
4 (A/AN) EMAIL / E-MAIL
5 STATISTICS / STATS
6 DESIGN
7 (BAR)(-)CHART
8 SPELLING ERROR / MISTAKE
9 MEDIA (STUDIES)
10 PROJECT TEAM
11 REFERENCES
12 SECTION HEADS

Part 2

13 F	14 G	15 A	16 C	17 E	18 C	19 F	20 H	21 E	22 G

Part 3

23 C	24 A	25 B	26 C	27 C	28 B	29 A	30 B

Tapescript

Listening Test 3

This is the Business English Certificate Vantage 5, Listening Test 3.

Part One. Questions 1 to 12.

You will hear three telephone conversations or messages.

Write one or two words or a number in the numbered spaces on the notes or forms below.

After you have listened once, replay each recording.

[pause]

Conversation One. Questions 1 to 4.

Look at the note below.

You will hear a man calling a colleague about making changes to his schedule.

You have 15 seconds to read through the notes.

[pause]

Now listen, and fill in the spaces.

[pause]

Woman:	Hello. Jackson's Associates.
Man:	Oh, hi! It's me, James. James Horrocks.
Woman:	Oh, James! Where <u>are</u> you?
Man:	I'm on the train – but I'm still in London! There's been a long delay and I'm going to be very late, so I'm going to have to reschedule my morning. Could you deal with it all for me?
Woman:	Sure . . .
Man:	I've got a meeting at half past ten with John Row of APF.
Woman:	What do you want me to do about it? Shall I try to get him to come later?

Man: That meeting will have to be cancelled or the whole morning's schedule will be impossible.
Woman: Right.
Man: Now, I'd also called a marketing meeting for eleven thirty. Could you give everyone a later time? Um, let's make it twelve thirty.
Woman: OK then.
Man: And as it'll be lunch time, could you call Jim Davis to arrange a lunch venue? People won't mind a late meeting if we offer them food!
Woman: OK.
Man: Oh, and, um, also, I won't have time to see Freda Bell when I finally get into the office. Could you email her for me? Otherwise, she'll think I've forgotten.
Woman: Fine. OK. Anything else?
Man: Nothing at the moment. See you soon, I hope.
Woman: OK. Bye . . .

[pause]

Now listen to the recording again.

[pause]

Conversation Two. Questions 5 to 8.

Look at the notes below.

You will hear a woman leaving a message for a colleague about his slides for a presentation.

You have 15 seconds to read through the notes.

[pause]

Now listen, and fill in the spaces.

[pause]

Hello, John, it's Christine. I've just looked through the revised slides for your presentation, and they're now much better. I've got a couple of general comments.
You thought there might be too many slides. I don't think that's a problem, though several would be improved if you replaced the statistics. A few words would be easier to take in.

Then don't the slides strike you as looking rather dull and predictable? The content is fine, but the design needs some variety. Maybe adding a few animations would help.

And two quite specific points. Something seems to have gone wrong in slide three. The graph is fine, but I can't make sense of the bar chart. It doesn't bear any relation to what's gone before, or after.

And finally, I remember we discussed the grammar mistake you had in slide six, and you've dealt with that, but if you have another look, I'm sure you'll notice the spelling error that's crept in.
OK, once you've dealt with that, it'll be fine. Goodbye.

[pause]

Now listen to the recording again.

[pause]

Conversation Three. Questions 9 to 12.

Look at the notes below.

You will hear a woman giving instructions to a colleague about dealing with job applications.

You have 15 seconds to read through the notes.

[pause]

Now listen, and fill in the spaces.

[pause]

Woman:	Hello?
Man:	It's Peter here from Personnel. The applications for the Publicity Co-ordinator post – how do you want us to sort them?
Woman:	First, could you look at the qualifications, and reject those who haven't done media studies. We can do IT training ourselves if necessary.
Man:	Right.
Woman:	Then the second time around, take a look at the Previous Experience section . . .
Man:	Yes.
Woman:	And pick out the ones who've worked as part of a project team before.
Man:	In a similar company?
Woman:	At this stage it doesn't matter whether it's in a service industry or any other kind.
Man:	OK. And did you want me to arrange interview dates yet? I'll need to book the rooms well ahead.
Woman:	I'll do that when you've decided on the final list. Before the interviews, can you get references for each of the candidates? Don't bother asking for copies of their certificates yet.
Man:	No problem . . . and what shall I do with their applications?
Woman:	Can you forward them to section heads? They'll probably sort them a bit more before they go to the marketing manager.
Man:	I'll do that before I . . .

[pause]

Now listen to the recording again.

[pause]

That is the end of Part One. You now have 20 seconds to check your answers.

[pause]

Part Two. Questions 13 to 22.

Section One. Questions 13 to 17.

You will hear five short recordings. Five people are giving advice on how to give feedback to employees.

For each recording, decide what advice the speaker gives.

Write one letter (A–H) next to the number of the recording.

Do not use any letter more than once.

After you have listened once, replay the recordings.

You have 15 seconds to read the list A–H.

[pause]

Now listen, and decide what advice each speaker gives.

[pause]

Thirteen
Basically the point of giving feedback is to motivate your staff to perform as well as they can in future. Nothing is a better motivator than telling someone that they are doing a wonderful job. I do not believe it could ever be the wrong time or place to draw attention to someone's plus points. So use your regular feedback sessions in this way to encourage your staff and make them feel good about themselves and their value to your company.

[pause]

Fourteen
When I started organising feedback sessions for my staff, I made the mistake of not letting them have their say. Although I'd criticise their performance tactfully, and I knew I had to do so immediately and in an appropriate place, I've now learned that it's sensible to allow them time to reflect – you can then agree to meet again at a later date if necessary. That means you've both had time to consider the implications of what's been said.

[pause]

Fifteen
Most employees feel they don't get enough feedback. On the rare occasions they *do* get it, it's either too superficial or it's because some kind of problem has arisen, and so it comes across as negative. The key to giving effective feedback is to allow a time for it each month, so that it becomes a matter of course, just part of the work routine. Then staff won't get nervous about it, and it'll be more positive.

[pause]

Sixteen
When a member of staff has made a serious mistake and you have no choice but to respond with serious negative feedback, then the best thing is to concentrate on what happened as a result of the criticised performance. That way your criticism will come across as reasoned and cannot be later dismissed by the employee as just your own unfair personal opinion. Don't just say that the work done was not satisfactory, but point out what effects it had.

[pause]

Seventeen
Sometimes when I was on the receiving end, I'd come out of feedback sessions with my boss wondering what on earth he'd been talking about. As a result, I always open sessions with my employee by saying something like 'I wanted to talk to you about the report you wrote yesterday'. I do this even when I'm responding on the spot to something that has just happened. It means we're both starting from the same point.

[pause]

Now listen to the recordings again.

[pause]

Section Two. Questions 18 to 22.

You will hear another five recordings. Five people are talking about their reasons for joining a particular company.

For each recording, decide why the speaker chose to join the company.

Write one letter (A–H) next to the number of the recording.

Do not use any letter more than once.

After you have listened once, replay the recordings.

You have 15 seconds to read the list A–H.

[pause]

Now listen, and decide why each speaker chose to join the company.

[pause]

Eighteen

I had really enjoyed working for my last company – I felt that I was really being given lots of different challenges especially in developing new products. But in the end, I felt they asked too much of me – I never seemed to have any time at home, and I felt I had to look around for another post. It was clear that this job would be much more manageable.

[pause]

Nineteen

I was lucky to be offered three different jobs. The interview for this one was quite a challenge – you know, the human resources manager was rather unwelcoming, I thought. But then we did a tour of the factory with several senior managers and saw all the different work areas. They seemed really go-ahead and talked a lot about their plans for the future etc. That decided it for me.

[pause]

Twenty

I really liked where I used to work because it was an extremely pleasant environment and I didn't have to commute any distance – unlike where I am now. But the thing was, I couldn't see myself being sufficiently challenged in the long run at my last place, whereas it was obvious in this current job description that if I stuck at the work, I could move up the company. And that's what I really wanted.

[pause]

Twenty-one

The job description sounded quite interesting, but I was a little worried that I wouldn't be able to fulfil all the criteria for the various aspects of the work – particularly the requirement to work as part of a large team. Anyway, I obviously managed to convince them at the interview I could do it, and I started last week. I'd actually been offered another job in a nearby firm, but I couldn't have lived so well on the remuneration package.

[pause]

Twenty-two

At my last place, I just didn't feel the environment was dynamic enough. I didn't feel I was going to be able to get ahead. I'm not so much interested in getting a higher or better paid position – or at least not yet – but I wanted my skills to be built up through a development programme. It was obvious at the interview that this company was very good in this respect.

[pause]

Now listen to the recordings again.

[pause]

That is the end of Part Two.

[pause]

Part Three. Questions 23 to 30.

You will hear the Chief Executive of Best Value, an American chain of convenience stores, talking about a change in the company's working practices.

For each question, 23–30, mark one letter (A, B or C) for the correct answer.

After you have listened once, replay the recording.

You have 45 seconds to read through the questions.

[pause]

Now listen, and mark A, B or C.

[pause]

Thank you very much for inviting me to talk to you about the introduction of Performance Management at Best Value.

Best Value operates nearly five thousand convenience stores and seven distribution centres in the United States. When I took over as Chief Executive, three years ago, I found poor industrial relations, and little or no sense of loyalty. A consultation process existed, but wasn't taken very seriously by management. Internal communications varied enormously, with a few staff missing out on key information.

We realised we had to do something to bring out the best in people, and we decided to adopt Performance Management to emphasise to the whole of our large workforce that there were many positive aspects to being one of our employees. If staff could develop a sense of fulfilment in their working days, we believed, it would both benefit them and be fundamental to the success of the rapid expansion we planned. We were convinced that in comparison, the effect of raising wages or reducing working hours would be minimal.

One decision we had to make was how to introduce Performance Management. We decided to start by focusing on a small number of units, but ones where we would have the greatest impact. And that meant the seven distribution centres, even though they presented more of a challenge than the stores. We felt that if we succeeded in raising morale there, it would have a knock-on effect on the stores.

So what is 'Performance Management'? It's a systematic, data-based approach to managing people, identifying the specific behaviours that we need from our staff and reinforcing those behaviours through recognition and reward. One of our first tasks was to identify the key behaviours needed to carry out the responsibilities of every post. This was the starting point for ensuring that each employee was best placed to use their own specific talents. I'm pleased to say it's working very well. Then we gave every employee a checklist of ten behaviours they need if they're going to perform their jobs well.

Managers and supervisors check each employee's performance at least once a day, and give them feedback and symbolic rewards – a variation on the gold star system. Staff are brought together to celebrate achievements by their unit and hear about each other's successes. We've realised that it isn't the results, but the social interaction and recognition that provide the real rewards for employees.

Let me give you an example of Performance Management in action. When we replaced our California distribution centre with a state-of-the-art facility, we decided to train all its managers in Performance Management before we took on any new staff. The managers then applied the approach when the centre was up and running, and achieved amazing results: average staff attendance at work was ninety-five per cent as opposed to around eighty-five per cent in other centres. This made it the most cost-effective by far.

In Texas, we have our first distribution centre established with completely new staff, and all the supervisors and managers were trained from the start in Performance Management principles. That centre now gets the right products to the right place at the right time, virtually one hundred per cent of the time. That's better than we've managed to achieve elsewhere, and contributes to the high degree of satisfaction in the stores it services.

With Performance Management, the desired behaviour becomes routine, so it gives a long-term payoff. And once employees understand their roles more clearly, and have changed the way they work, it's much easier to agree on realistic objectives. This makes it less likely that the company has to cut costs, or take other emergency measures.

To round off, let me say that Performance Management has really transformed Best Value. And the important thing to remember is that it works for everyone.

[pause]

Now listen to the recording again.

[pause]

That is the end of Part Three. You now have ten minutes to transfer your answers to your Answer Sheet.

[pause]

Note: Teacher, stop the recording here and time ten minutes. Remind students when there is **one** minute remaining.

That is the end of the test.

Test 4   Reading

Part 1

1 C   2 A   3 D   4 B   5 C   6 A   7 D

Part 2

8 B   9 E   10 A   11 F   12 D

Part 3

13 A   14 B   15 B   16 D   17 D   18 C

Part 4

19 D   20 A   21 B   22 C   23 B   24 C   25 B   26 B
27 D   28 A   29 B   30 C   31 B   32 D   33 A

Part 5

34 ARE   35 BEEN   36 IT   37 LIKE   38 MAKE   39 SO
40 CORRECT   41 THEM   42 CORRECT   43 IN   44 WHICH   45 FROM

Test 4   Writing

Part 1

Sample A

> I'd like to inform you that the annual conference will take place on 20th, 12, 2010. It's very important for your attending because we'll talk about the plan for recruitment next year during the meeting. If you prepare a presentation, please show it in the type of PPT.

Scales	Mark	Commentary
Content	5	All content is relevant to the task and the target reader would be fully informed.
Communicative Achievement	3	Uses email conventions to hold the reader's attention. The register and tone are appropriate for an email (*I'd like to inform you …*). The text communicates straightforward ideas to the target reader.
Organisation	3	The email is well-organised using a variety of organisational features, e.g. linking words (*because*) and pronominal referencing (*please show it*).
Language	4	Uses a range of vocabulary (*take place*; *recruitment*) and both simple and complex grammatical forms (*If you prepare … please …*). Errors are minimal (*in the type of PPT*).

Sample B

> Dear Human Resources managers,
> I would like to inform you that the annual conference will be held at 10:00am this Friday. The subject is about the training courses for new staffs. please noted that you must offer a specific training courses plan for the aboave.
> Wish every manage can make a presentation on time. Thanks.
> HR Dept.

Scales	Mark	Commentary
Content	2	The second content element has to be inferred. The third content element is unclear and the target reader would be only partially informed (*Wish every manage can make a presentation on time*).
Communicative Achievement	3	Uses email conventions to hold the reader's attention and communicate straightforward ideas (*the annual conference will be held …*).
Organisation	3	The text is well-organised and coherent.
Language	2	Uses some everyday business vocabulary (*training courses*) and some complex grammatical forms (*I would like to inform you that*; *you must offer*). Errors are noticeable but meaning can still be determined (*new staffs*; *please noted*; *every manage*).

Part 2

Sample C

> Proposal: "New York store"
>
> After reviewing the activities of our NY store, some measures seem to be necessary to improve the performance of the store and keep it open:
>
> — First of all, we should cut the cost of running the store by optimising the logistics of the store.
>
> — Additionally, the store manager should be replaced and some team building activities should be conducted because the staff is very unhappy with the present management.
>
> — in order to rise sales again, we should invest on the one hand in some advertising and on the other hand in a new store design. This might also improve the poor store image.
>
> All measures should start as soon as possible because otherwise we may have to close this very good located store.

Scales	Mark	Commentary
Content	5	All content is relevant and expanded where appropriate. The target reader would be fully informed.
Communicative Achievement	5	The format, tone and register are all appropriate to the conventions of a proposal (*After reviewing*; *All measures should start*) and would have a positive effect on the target reader.
Organisation	5	The proposal is well-organised and coherent, with effective use of a variety of organisational features, including bullet points and cohesive devices, e.g. linkers (*First of all*; *Additionally*; *on the one hand … on the other hand*) and referencing (*keep it open*; *This might …*).
Language	5	The proposal uses a good range of grammatical structures and vocabulary (*optimising the logistics*; *team building activities should be conducted*; *otherwise we may have to …*). Errors are minimal and do not impede communication (*to rise sales*; *this very good located store*).

Sample D

Recommendations for the store

I have read some information about the New York store now. It has some troubles but it doesn't matter.

The New York store is in a very good location. This is a big advantage, so it should be kept open.

The high cost of running store is the biggest issue. In my opinion, we should fire some staff to reduce the cost.

From the information I know the staff are unhappy. Therefore, we should build a lively atmosphere. For instance, we should communicate with the staff. Secondly, let green plants all around us is also a great idea. Both will work to make staff fell better.

How can we to improve the sales. The discount should be taken into account.

At last we need a new store design and that's all.

Scales	Mark	Commentary
Content	4	All the content is relevant and the target reader would be informed but some of the content is not fully expanded e.g. content element 5.
Communicative Achievement	3	Generally uses the conventions of a proposal effectively to hold the reader's attention, although there are some inconsistencies in register (*but it doesn't matter*; *and that's all*).
Organisation	3	The proposal is well-organised with a range of linking words (*Therefore*; *Secondly*) and use of pronouns to avoid repetition (*the New York store … It has some troubles*).
Language	3	Uses a range of lexis and structures (*the biggest issue*; *we should build a lively atmosphere*). There are a number of errors (*has some troubles*; *of running store*; *let green plants all around*) but these do not impede communication.

Test 4   Listening

Part 1

1 WARE(-)HOUSE (GATE)
2 (SECURITY) IDS / ID (CARD(S))
3 MANUAL
4 PARKING AREA
5 AIR(-)CONDITIONING
6 (THE) QUALITY (CONTROL)
7 ASSEMBLY LINE
8 COMPENSATION
9 CASE STUDY
10 FONT
11 SCREEN
12 (BODY) MOVEMENT

Part 2

13 E   14 A   15 G   16 D   17 C   18 D   19 C   20 A   21 G   22 H

Part 3

23 C   24 C   25 B   26 C   27 B   28 A   29 B   30 A

Tapescript

Listening Test 4

This is the Business English Certificate Vantage 5, Listening Test 4.

Part One. Questions 1 to 12.

You will hear three telephone conversations or messages.

Write one or two words or a number in the numbered spaces on the notes or forms below.

After you have listened once, replay each recording.

[pause]

Conversation One. Questions 1 to 4.

Look at the note below.

You will hear a man leaving a message about deliveries for one of his company's suppliers.

You have 15 seconds to read through the note.

[pause]

Now listen, and fill in the spaces.

[pause]

Good morning. This is Gupta Ramesh from Morgan and Turnbull. We've been having a few security problems lately, so we've reviewed our delivery arrangements. First of all, until further notice, drivers should use the warehouse gate instead of the main factory gate. That's the one in Station Road.

A second point I want to discuss is – as you have heard – we're issuing IDs to replace the general permits drivers are using at the moment. We're sending couriers with them tomorrow morning. They should be placed on the inside of the windscreen to activate the sensor in the gate. It's very important they don't forget to do it because after this week there'll only be automatic access to the yard – we're putting a stop to manual access. And finally – this is a safety measure to reduce vehicle movement in the yard – in future drivers should proceed to the parking area before checking in at reception. I hope this is all clear. Please call me if you have any problem. Bye.

[pause]

Now listen to the recording again.

[pause]

Conversation Two. Questions 5 to 8.

Look at the form below.

You will hear a woman phoning an architect to discuss a problem with a building project.

You have 15 seconds to read through the form.

[pause]

Now listen, and fill in the spaces.

[pause]

Man:	Hello, Frank Bauer speaking.
Woman:	Hello this is Antonia Radford from Speedlink. I'm phoning about a problem with our extension project at the factory.
Man:	Ah. I thought everything was on schedule . . .
Woman:	So did I, until today. I called the site foreman because the air conditioning was due to be put in this week, but the subcontractors weren't there. They'd left a message that everything was on hold.
Man:	What reason did they give?
Woman:	I thought it'd be a transport delay because the system's coming from the States. Apparently though, there's a hold up at the supplier's end, a quality control issue at the plant, actually.
Man:	I see.
Woman:	Now, as you know, the rest of the construction work is more or less finished, but we can't start the assembly line until this system is operational for health and safety reasons. We were due to begin production next week . . .
Man:	Right. That's why we drew up a contract that allowed you to claim compensation in these circumstances.
Woman:	Absolutely. So could you please inform the building company we will be expecting that for each day's further delay.

[pause]

Now listen to the recording again.

[pause]

Conversation Three. Questions 9 to 12.

Look at the notes below.

You will hear a woman giving feedback to a colleague on his presentation at a conference.

You have 15 seconds to read through the notes.

[pause]

Now listen, and fill in the spaces.

[pause]

Woman:	Hello John, it's Kim. You wanted some advice about your presentation.
Man:	Please. That's the first time I've given it and I'm repeating it next month.
Woman:	Well, the introduction was clear and you finished on time without appearing hurried. The case study you analysed seemed a bit long though.
Man:	You're right. I'll cut it a bit.
Woman:	Now the slides – you had the right amount. Personally, I'd use a larger font though – it helps in a big hall. But the graphs made your point well.
Man:	Good. I worked hard at those.
Woman:	Another tip – you didn't turn your back on the audience – but be careful not to block their view of the screen – it's frustrating if they can't see what the presenter's referring to.
Man:	I was so nervous.
Woman:	You didn't sound it. You spoke very clearly. Think about your body language though. You don't want to stand absolutely still, but avoid too much movement if you can.
Man:	That's really helpful.
Woman:	You're welcome.

[pause]

Now listen to the recording again.

[pause]

That is the end of Part One. You now have 20 seconds to check your answers.

[pause]

Part Two. Questions 13 to 22.

Section One. Questions 13 to 17.

You will hear five short recordings. Five people are explaining why they rejected a candidate for a job.

For each recording, decide why the speaker rejected the candidate.

Write one letter (A–H) next to the number of the recording.

Do not use any letter more than once.

After you have listened once, replay the recordings.

You have 15 seconds to read the list A–H.

[pause]

Now listen, and decide why each speaker rejected the candidate.

[pause]

Thirteen
I thought he was a very interesting candidate with wide experience who would probably work effectively, despite not having been to university. However, this job requires someone who can work closely with colleagues, and I'm not quite sure he'd be the team-player we want. Although, he's got possible leadership qualities, I think he'd be better in a job where he can make his own decisions, and that's not what we want for this position.

[pause]

Fourteen
Well, she showed a lot of enthusiasm and ambition, and I liked the way she presented herself and expressed her ideas. Because she'd be working with young people, her youth would be an advantage.

However, that's not enough for this job which needs someone who's already worked in the industry, so the fact that she hasn't goes against her. She'd probably be the ideal candidate in a few years' time once she's got the right track record.

[pause]

Fifteen
She was a difficult person to interview, although once she got going her answers were very interesting. But in this business, we need young people who can express themselves assertively and clearly. It's a pity, because her background is very suitable – especially her ability to work alone and her qualifications. The salary we're offering was also very acceptable to her, but I don't believe she would be very good in face-to-face situations.

[pause]

Sixteen
He's certainly got the determination to succeed. He's definitely very experienced in the field, and the MBA would have been an added bonus. He's very keen to get to the top of his profession, so I don't think he'd be content staying in one job for any length of time, and that could be a problem for us. If he aims to reach the top by the time he's thirty, he'll need experience of several companies.

[pause]

Seventeen
He was a strange candidate. Lots of experience in the industry according to his CV, although he hadn't got a degree, which is surprising considering the positions he's held before. And he's hoping to lead a team, but I don't think he showed enough determination or interest to work without supervision. He said he wants to leave his current job because he's bored there.

[pause]

Now listen to the recordings again.

[pause]

Section Two. Questions 18 to 22.

You will hear another five recordings. Five people are giving their opinion about the annual performance review process in their companies.

For each recording, decide what the speaker thought about the performance review process.

Write one letter (A–H) next to the number of the recording.

Do not use any letter more than once.

After you have listened once, replay the recordings.

You have 15 seconds to read the list A–H.

[pause]

Now listen, and decide what each speaker thought about the performance review process.

[pause]

Eighteen
My company's been doing annual appraisals for all employees ever since I started here. I thought it was a waste of time at first, just another boring thing to do. But I appreciate it now. In my appraisal, I looked back over the year and saw what I'd achieved, and that helped my belief in myself. Without the annual appraisal, I think time would slip by without my ever getting a real idea of my worth to the company.

[pause]

Nineteen

Most of my colleagues hate the annual appraisal. They're afraid of criticism and worried about what sort of information will go on their file – so they can't see the value of the whole thing. Not me. I've just had my latest interview, and I spent weeks planning it. Promotion is awarded according to a points system in my firm, but there's room for manoeuvre, and the appraisal is an opportunity to work your way onto the next step up the ladder.

[pause]

Twenty

I'm a line manager, and I've just carried out the latest lot of appraisals for my staff. It's very time-consuming and difficult for me. I get on well with my team, and I don't want to spoil my relationship with them by saying the wrong thing. But nobody's perfect, and the appraisals have improved productivity by getting people to do something about their weaknesses. Constructive criticism is the key, but finding the right words is a problem.

[pause]

Twenty-one

When annual appraisals first became general practice, we were pretty bad at it. As personnel manager, I called the staff into my office for a ten-minute chat – there was some form to fill in, and that was it. But nowadays a lot of thought goes into the process, and the last round of appraisals was treated very seriously. I used questionnaires constructed to build up a profile of each employee – so I could make informed decisions regarding training, promotion etc.

[pause]

Twenty-two

Appraisals have to be a positive encounter. And they must be confidential, if the employees are to trust the process enough to be open. I'm a manager – when it comes to appraisals, my policy is to keep the initial review part short, and spend longer discussing future projects. I treated my last lot of appraisals as a sort of question and answer session with my staff. Not everything that came out of the interviews was practical, but it was interesting to hear what they thought.

[pause]

Now listen to the recordings again.

[pause]

That is the end of Part Two.

[pause]

Part Three. Questions 23 to 30.

You will hear Desmond Butler, owner of Klikset, talking about how he created a successful toy company.

For each question, 23–30, mark one letter (A, B or C) for the correct answer.

After you have listened once, replay the recording.

You have 45 seconds to read through the questions.

[pause]

Now listen, and mark A, B or C.

[pause]

Woman: Today I'm talking to Desmond Butler, Managing Director of Klikset, the construction toy which every youngster wants. Welcome Desmond.

Man:	Hello Jenny.
Woman:	So, how did it all start?
Man:	I'd been running my father's plastic component business and I'd taken it as far as I could, and was bored. We were producing make-up cases – you know, eye-shadow, lipstick, mascara cases and so on. It was a steady market, although very competitive, but I needed a new challenge. I was getting quite a good income from it, but money isn't everything.
Woman:	So what gave you the idea for Klikset?
Man:	I was at a wedding party, sitting in a corner toying with plastic drinking straws on my table thinking about the manufacturing process that made them. I began piecing them together and managed to build a small flat structure. I realised that with the right connectors I could build some impressive objects and I thought this might be the seed idea for a new toy.
Woman:	How did you plan to get started?
Man:	Well, my initial idea was to develop the toy and sell the concept to a big toy company. I would then retain the contract to make it and get them to sell it under their brand name. I didn't know anything about the toy market and thought it'd be better to leave the selling to the experts.
Woman:	Did it take long to get a prototype ready?
Man:	Longer than I'd anticipated. I spent eighteen months refining the straw idea with six lengths of rod connectors before the basic Klikset was ready. Once I'd decided to go down the path that was it. Nothing was going to stop me. If it was a total failure, it would set me back five years financially, but I believed it would catch on eventually.
Woman:	So did you go ahead and set up your company then?
Man:	I tried to sell it to the big manufacturers, who didn't want to know. I decided that as they weren't interested, I would learn their business and do it myself. I researched the toy industry thoroughly. I even applied for jobs in toy shops just so I could go to the interviews and find out more about the business. I also contacted as many store buyers as possible and asked what kind of toys they were looking for. I got a part-time job in a toy factory before setting up Klikset in nineteen ninety-three.
Woman:	And was it easy to sell your product?
Man:	At first, no. The biggest toy store initially turned me down, but finally I saw their chief buyer Jim Taylor. He liked my business plan, but told me that what I had to offer probably had zero value to him. So I asked for five minutes to do a presentation and I pulled out all the stops. I made a Ferris wheel, a windmill and a bulldozer and within a couple of minutes Jim Taylor was won over. I sold one million pounds worth of toys through his store that first year.
Woman:	An amazing success story. But it didn't stop there, did it?
Man:	No. Elto, one of the companies which had turned me down initially, contacted me and said they were interested in my designs after all. So I negotiated a deal with them to form a partnership to make Klikset and market it abroad. I even persuaded them to buy ten per cent of my business for ten million pounds. They wanted a fifty-fifty partnership but I wanted to keep control of my business.
Woman:	Finally, Desmond, what do you put your success down to?
Man:	Well, however much you plan you can never be sure how things will turn out. You have to make decisions and just live with the consequences. I've always learnt something from my mistakes.
Woman:	Well thank you Desmond for your wonderful . . .

[pause]

Now listen to the recording again.

[pause]

That is the end of Part Three. You now have ten minutes to transfer your answers to your Answer Sheet.

[pause]

Note: Teacher, stop the recording here and time ten minutes. Remind students when there is **one** minute remaining.

That is the end of the test.

INTERLOCUTOR FRAMES

To facilitate practice for the Speaking test, the scripts followed by the interlocutor for Parts 2 and 3 appear below. They should be used in conjunction with Tests 1–4 Speaking tasks. These tasks are contained in booklets in the real Speaking test.

Interlocutor frames are not included for Part 1, in which the interlocutor asks the candidates questions directly rather than asking them to perform tasks.

Part 2: Mini presentations (about six minutes)

Interlocutor:
- Now, in this part of the test I'm going to give each of you a choice of three different topics. I'd like you to select one of the topics and give a short presentation on it for about a minute. You will have a minute to prepare this and you can make notes if you wish. After you have finished your talk, your partner will ask you a question.
- All right? Here are your topics. Please don't write anything in the booklet.

[Interlocutor hands each candidate a booklet and a pencil and paper for notes.]

Interlocutor:
- Now, *B*, which topic have you chosen, A, B or C?
- Would you like to talk about what you think is important when *[interlocutor states candidate's chosen topic]*? *A*, please listen carefully to *B*'s talk and then ask him/her a question about it.

[Candidate B speaks for one minute.]

Interlocutor:
- Thank you. Now, *A*, please ask *B* a question about his/her talk.

[Candidate A asks a question.]

Interlocutor:
- Now, *A*, which topic have you chosen, A, B or C?
- Would you like to talk about what you think is important when *[interlocutor states candidate's chosen topic]*? *B*, please listen carefully to *A*'s talk and then ask him/her a question about it.

[Candidate A speaks for one minute.]

Interlocutor:
- Thank you. Now, *B*, please ask *A* a question about his/her talk.

[Candidate B asks a question.]

Interlocutor:
- Thank you.
- Can I have the booklets, please?

Part 3: Collaborative task and discussion (about seven minutes)

Interlocutor:
- Now, in this part of the test, you are going to discuss something together.

[Interlocutor holds the Part 3 booklet open at the task while giving the instructions below.]

Interlocutor:
- You have 30 seconds to read this task carefully, and then about three minutes to discuss and decide about it together. You should give reasons for your decisions and opinions. You don't need to write anything. Is that clear?

[Interlocutor places the booklet in front of the candidates so they can both see it.]

Interlocutor:
- I'm just going to listen and then ask you to stop after about three minutes. Please speak so that we can hear you.

[Candidates have about three minutes to complete the task.]

Interlocutor:
• Can I have the booklet, please?

[Interlocutor asks one or more of the follow-on questions as appropriate, to extend the discussion.]

• Thank you. That is the end of the test.

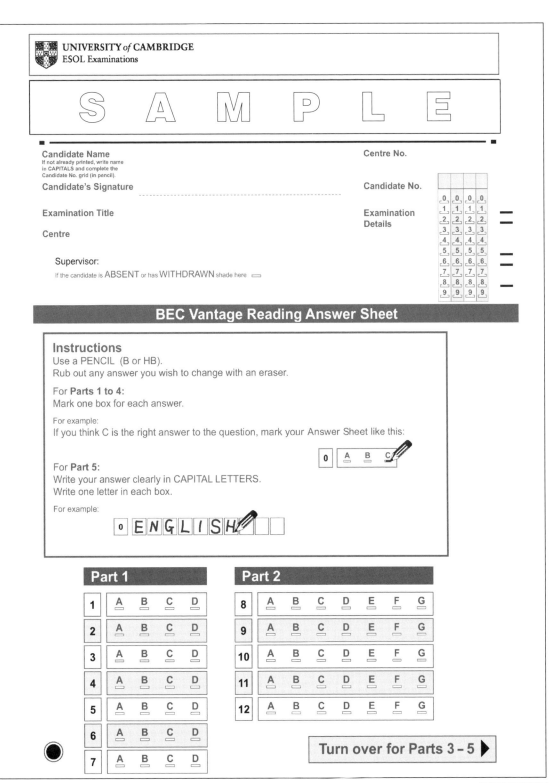

Part 3

13	A	B	C	D
14	A	B	C	D
15	A	B	C	D
16	A	B	C	D
17	A	B	C	D
18	A	B	C	D

Part 4

19	A	B	C	D
20	A	B	C	D
21	A	B	C	D
22	A	B	C	D
23	A	B	C	D
24	A	B	C	D
25	A	B	C	D
26	A	B	C	D

27	A	B	C	D
28	A	B	C	D
29	A	B	C	D
30	A	B	C	D
31	A	B	C	D
32	A	B	C	D
33	A	B	C	D

Part 5

34		1 34 0
35		1 35 0
36		1 36 0
37		1 37 0
38		1 38 0
39		1 39 0
40		1 40 0
41		1 41 0
42		1 42 0
43		1 43 0
44		1 44 0
45		1 45 0

UNIVERSITY *of* CAMBRIDGE
ESOL Examinations

SAMPLE

Candidate Name
If not already printed, write name
in CAPITALS and complete the
Candidate No. grid (in pencil).

Candidate's Signature

Examination Title

Centre

Supervisor:

If the candidate is ABSENT or has WITHDRAWN shade here

Centre No.

Candidate No.

Examination Details

0	0	0	0
1	1	1	1
2	2	2	2
3	3	3	3
4	4	4	4
5	5	5	5
6	6	6	6
7	7	7	7
8	8	8	8
9	9	9	9

BEC Vantage Listening Answer Sheet

Instructions
Use a PENCIL (B or HB).
Rub out any answer you wish to change with an eraser.

For **Part 1:**
Write your answer clearly in CAPITAL LETTERS.
Write one letter or number in each box.
If the answer has more than one word, leave one box empty between words.

For example:

| 0 | Q | U | E | S | T | I | O | N | | 1 | 2 | | |

For **Parts 2 and 3:**
Mark one box for each answer.

For example:
If you think C is the right answer to the question, mark your Answer Sheet like this:

| 0 | A | B | C |

Part 1 - Conversation One

1

1 1 0

2

1 2 0

3

1 3 0

4

1 4 0

Continue on the other side of this sheet ▶

© UCLES 2012 Photocopiable

Part 1 - Conversation Two

5 | | | | | | | | | | | | | | | | | | | | | | | | | | | | |

1 5 0

6 | | | | | | | | | | | | | | | | | | | | | | | | | | | | |

1 6 0

7 | | | | | | | | | | | | | | | | | | | | | | | | | | | | |

1 7 0

8 | | | | | | | | | | | | | | | | | | | | | | | | | | | | |

1 8 0

Part 1 - Conversation Three

9 | | | | | | | | | | | | | | | | | | | | | | | | | | | | |

1 9 0

10 | | | | | | | | | | | | | | | | | | | | | | | | | | | | |

1 10 0

11 | | | | | | | | | | | | | | | | | | | | | | | | | | | | |

1 11 0

12 | | | | | | | | | | | | | | | | | | | | | | | | | | | | |

1 12 0

Part 2 - Section One

13	A	B	C	D	E	F	G	H
14	A	B	C	D	E	F	G	H
15	A	B	C	D	E	F	G	H
16	A	B	C	D	E	F	G	H
17	A	B	C	D	E	F	G	H

Part 2 - Section Two

18	A	B	C	D	E	F	G	H
19	A	B	C	D	E	F	G	H
20	A	B	C	D	E	F	G	H
21	A	B	C	D	E	F	G	H
22	A	B	C	D	E	F	G	H

Part 3

23	A	B	C
24	A	B	C
25	A	B	C
26	A	B	C
27	A	B	C
28	A	B	C
29	A	B	C
30	A	B	C